NYSTCE®

School Building Leader Practice Questions

DEAR FUTURE EXAM SUCCESS STORY

First of all, **THANK YOU** for purchasing Mometrix study materials!

Second, congratulations! You are one of the few determined test-takers who are committed to doing whatever it takes to excel on your exam. **You have come to the right place.** We developed these practice tests with one goal in mind: to deliver you the best possible approximation of the questions you will see on test day.

Standardized testing is one of the biggest obstacles on your road to success, which only increases the importance of doing well in the high-pressure, high-stakes environment of test day. Your results on this test could have a significant impact on your future, and these practice tests will give you the repetitions you need to build your familiarity and confidence with the test content and format to help you achieve your full potential on test day.

Your success is our success

We would love to hear from you! If you would like to share the story of your exam success or if you have any questions or comments in regard to our products, please contact us at **800-673-8175** or **support@mometrix.com**.

Thanks again for your business and we wish you continued success!

Sincerely,
The Mometrix Test Preparation Team

Printed in the United States of America

TABLE OF CONTENTS

Practice Test #1

Multiple Choice Questions

1. How should school leaders and others analyze school data to inform the school vision?

a. Across grade levels instead of across school years.
b. By subject matter rather than by student cohorts.
c. By formative and summative assessment findings.
d. By teachers within grades instead of across levels.

2. Which of the following is accurate about the uses of data in goal-related activities?

a. Qualitative data is not useful when setting goals aligned with school vision and mission.
b. Data connected to vision and mission enable monitoring progress for goals.
c. Only formative data is relevant to how schools allocate resources to meet their goals.
d. Formal data collection is not necessary to assess family and community relations.

3. Of the following, which is an advantage of developing a school vision collaboratively?

a. Visions developed through collaboration can be implemented far faster.
b. Visions are clearer and more coherent when developed by collaboration.
c. Visions take longer times in the process of development, slowing change.
d. Visions tend to be more appropriate to their local school district contexts.

4. Which of the following is NOT true about the qualifications of teachers in public schools?

a. Teachers must be fully-certified to teach in a public school.
b. Teachers must be highly-qualified to teach in a public school.
c. A teacher who moves states may have to demonstrate subject-matter competency in the new state to teach.
d. Teachers in high-performing schools generally have more qualifications than teachers in other public schools.

5. Which of the following statements is most accurate about how school leaders align school policies and practices with federal, state, district, and local school system policies?

a. State standardized assessment instruments are based solely on standards developed by states.
b. Individual schools directly apply state standards for developing their standardized assessments.
c. Schools directly reflect system standards, and yet ultimately are also aligned with federal policy.
d. Local school districts develop standardized assessments applying the federal standards directly.

6. Which of the following is true regarding how school leaders can foster equitable and inclusive educational practices?

a. The development of curriculum should solely be based on developmental appropriateness.
b. School leaders should model respect for diversity and offer multiple means for celebrating it.
c. Involving culturally diverse community stakeholders in school decisions is the responsibility of the school district.

d. Only school leaders are accountable to ensure equity for every student in all school programs.

7. Which of the following is a primary benefit of distributed leadership?

a. Distributed leadership helps to maintain status quo, especially in high-performing schools.
b. School leaders who practice distributive leadership are less stressed because they are able to delegate responsibilities.
c. Practicing distributive leadership builds capacity in others and develops followers into leaders.
d. Distributive leadership helps to identify weak team members that need to be replaced.

8. Which of the following statements is not accurate about requirements for integrating technology comprehensively into instruction to support school vision?

a. Successful school-wide implementation of educational technology is dependent on the technology selected, not school leadership.
b. Regardless of the technology capabilities of school staff, training and professional development are needed to successfully implement educational technology school-wide.
c. School structure and organization impact the success of adopting educational technology.
d. Schools must have the resources and support for implementing technology school-wide.

9. The National Education Association (NEA) Code of Ethics principle of Commitment to the Student prohibits which of the following actions?

a. Encouraging students to learn of various perspectives independently.
b. Reasonable efforts to safeguard students against harmful conditions.
c. Disclosing student information which is pertinent to student progress.
d. Disclosing student information if not legally or professionally required.

10. Which of the following is a practice of a school leader that facilitates family involvement in education?

a. Hiring parent facilitators using state Title I and Smart Start funds.
b. Working extended hours on campus.
c. Collaborating with parents who are already involved in school activities.
d. Sending an e-newsletter to parents weekly.

11. Compared to majority rule and committees, what is a more salient characteristic of group consensus as a way of making collaborative educational decisions?

a. It is more time-efficient than these other methods.
b. It can undermine commitment for minority voters.
c. It is more thorough and hears all members' voices.
d. It may make member time and effort not worth it.

12. Challenges to school leaders for promoting student mental health include limited resources. Among such limitations, which is most related to federal accountability mandates?

a. Ratios of school counselors to students.
b. School counselor responsibility change.
c. Inadequate support staff development.
d. Districts' mental health staff budgeting.

13. In public school districts, which personnel are *not* likely to be directly supervised by the campus principal?

a. Bus drivers.
b. Custodians.
c. Volunteers.
d. Cafeteria workers.

14. To build a positive culture of learning and high expectations, school leaders can guide teachers to identify instructional activities that are aligned to the curriculum and have been proven to be effective. Which of the following is an indicator of effective implementation of instructional activities?

a. Differentiated instruction.
b. Increased student attendance.
c. Flexible student grouping.
d. Focused discussions and effective interaction between students.

15. Which of the following should be considered first when adopting curriculum?

a. Alignment to federal and state standards.
b. Teacher approval.
c. Community approval.
d. Board approval.

16. What should school leaders keep in mind when integrating technology into standards-based curricula?

a. They should assign their teachers to write technology standards.
b. They cannot help students meet standards by using technology.
c. They do not need to require students to master technology standards.
d. They should focus on learning with technology, not learning about it.

17. Which of the following principles about formative assessment should school leaders consider when giving feedback to and collaborating with teachers?

a. Student motivation and learning are unaffected by assessment types.
b. Student motivation and learning are affected by assessment types.
c. Error is inevitable in all assessment, and only summative assessment is a valid indicator of student learning.
d. Student performance against a standard is more important than student growth.

18. Which of the following is not accurate regarding school leaders' engagement of faculty and staff in ongoing self-assessment and improvement?

a. To encourage self-direction in improving, leaders should model self-assessment and improvement.
b. To encourage self-direction in improving, leaders should actively engage workers.
c. To encourage self-direction in improving, leaders should make learning accessible.
d. To encourage self-direction in improving, leaders should leave self-improvement up to employees.

19. A school leader is looking to incorporate daily effort into professional development in a collaborative way across the campus. Which of the following professional development and learning opportunities is NOT collaborative in nature and useful for daily teacher activities?

a. Conducting action research
b. Professional learning communities (PLCs)
c. Daily reading of professional research in journal publications
d. Structured observations

20. Which instructional materials would most promote student reflection?

a. Textbook end-of-chapter study questions.
b. Venn diagrams and other graphic organizers.
c. Journals for students to write in regularly.
d. Worksheets for exercising new learning.

21. Which pedagogical shift best supports the integration of technology into instructional practice?

a. From homogenous student groups to heterogenous student groups.
b. From learning passively to learning actively.
c. From teacher-directed learning to student-paced learning.
d. From lesson activities to project-based learning.

22. Which of the following practices best represents the least restrictive environment (LRE) for a student who receives special education services?

a. The student remains in a classroom with other students who receive special education services throughout the day, with the exception of ancillary classes.
b. The student attends classes with students who do not receive special education services, but reports to a special education teacher's classroom during independent practice of each core class.
c. The student reports to a special education teacher's classroom for math and reading only.
d. The student attends classes with students who do not receive special education services and classroom teachers provide modifications to the curriculum and/or accommodations to assist the student.

23. Which of the following is correct about effective classroom management systems?

a. Tiered positive behavior support models provide both prevention and intervention.
b. Tiered positive behavior support models are only for preventing behavior problems.
c. Tiered positive behavior support models are designed to be behavior interventions.
d. Tiered positive behavior support models provide less time in academic engagement.

24. Which of the following statements is true about a school climate in which students feel supported?

a. Students find resources and support are readily available to them.
b. Students who share multiple classes are more likely to form relationships with one another.
c. Student roles and responsibilities are clearly defined in policy handbooks.
d. Student feelings of support are not affected by interactions with adults.

25. Which of the following is the best example of differentiated instruction based on product?

a. Teach different content for different students.
b. Allow students to choose between writing an essay or recording a video for an assignment.
c. Give students different version of assessments.
d. Assign some students to watch a video while others read an article.

26. Which of the following actions best demonstrates that a principal makes decisions to improve instruction based on evidence from student data?

a. Meeting with parents frequently during grading periods.
b. Conducting meetings for Professional Learning Committees based on grade levels and subject areas.
c. Requiring teachers to host tutorial sessions for students after the regular school day.
d. Submitting reports to district office personnel after each grading period.

27. Which of the following is true regarding best practices for school leaders when giving teachers observational feedback?

a. Leaders should give feedback statements rather than asking questions.
b. Leaders should disregard strengths to focus on improving weaknesses.
c. Leaders should emphasize all identified areas for improvement equally.
d. Leaders should include some specific next steps attainable for teachers.

28. Which of the following would most impact the success of a new teacher induction program?

a. Providing optional coaching sessions for new teachers.
b. Assigning mentors to new teachers based on the seniority of the mentor teacher.
c. Providing opportunities for collaboration and leadership development.
d. The school leader facilitates all aspects of the induction program.

29. Which of the following should school principals primarily look for when observing teachers in classrooms for evaluation purposes?

a. They should focus on what students want to learn rather than what they want them to learn.
b. They should look for how comfortable the teacher is with the lesson content and method of delivery.
c. They should look for evidence of learning such as student responses to checks for understanding and student work products.
d. They should focus on physical classroom setup.

30. Which of the following have education researchers identified as important regarding implementation of school-wide data initiatives??

a. More training opportunities and promotion of the data system in implementation are most effective.
b. Technology that supports data initiatives offers the answer to data use in schools.
c. Individual teachers utilize data technology systems more quickly and productively.
d. The success of a school data initiative is determined by the data system selected.

31. In terms of assessment, which of the following is a true statement that school leaders should consider when minimizing bias and maximizing equity for all students?

a. Accommodations given to students during testing are inherently unfair.
b. Progress monitoring using student data decreases achievement gaps.
c. Achievement gaps can be resolved by testing low performing students frequently and extensively.
d. Assessment validity and reliability nullifies most non-standardized test results.

32. The Federal Departments of Education and Justice collaborated to produce a package (2014) offering guidance for legal and fair disciplinary decisions, policies, and practices. What is most accurate about the intents of this guidance?

a. It aims to lower overrepresentation of minority students in expulsion and suspension rates.
b. It is meant to help schools establish positive learning environments, rather than focus on school safety.
c. It is primarily intended to reduce violent school incidents in response to rising rates of school violence.
d. It aims to make behavioral interventions federally legal rather than non-discriminatory.

33. Which of the following accurately represents how school leaders can promote equitable access to curriculum for all students and their parents?

a. They can make staff more comfortable in discussing diversity without promoting equity.
b. They can clarify school staff misconceptions related to deficit theories about minorities.
c. They can model equity in daily interactions, but should avoid confronting discrimination.
d. They can create safe environments, though student support networks are not their job.

34. Which of these is true regarding school leader efforts involving school improvement plans, policies, and structures to improve parent engagement, student engagement, and student achievement?

a. School improvement plans increased parental meeting attendance but not student school attendance.
b. School improvement plans decreased student behavior problems while increasing their achievement.
c. Central office policies and structures increased parent engagement in individual schools, not systems.
d. School improvement plans increased student enrollment and achievement, not parent involvement.

35. Which of the following statements is most accurate about why schools must collaborate with their communities in providing mental health services to remove learning barriers and improve student outcomes?

a. In many communities and states, schools are often children's only mental health service providers.
b. Due to stigma associated with mental health needs, parents avoid familiar school settings and staff.
c. According to research study findings, students are less likely to seek counseling services in schools.
d. Mental health services in schools should be separated from mental health services in communities.

36. In school change processes, which of these is an example of a first-order change?

a. Forming a different approach to instruction.
b. Forming new interactions and relationships.
c. Forming site-based school advisory councils.
d. Forming a sense of collaborative ownership.

37. In reference to the Supportive School Discipline Initiative (SSDI), former US Attorney General Eric Holder said a federal initiative to guide school disciplinary practices would "make schools safe, supportive and inclusive for all students" and would "keep America's young people safe and on the right path." How did he say it would do these things?

a. By making discipline less exclusionary.
b. By divorcing discipline from civil rights.
c. By getting data from resource officers.
d. By referring discipline to peace officers.

38. In school-wide positive behavior support (SPBS) programs, which of the following is a procedure associated with tier 3?

a. Socio-emotional groups.
b. Daily check-in and check-out.
c. Intervention family support.
d. Individualized interventions.

39. Which of the following strategies for implementing technology is most closely related to leadership in implementing a school improvement plan?

a. Utilizing technology as a tool to facilitate collaboration among staff.
b. Utilizing technology as a tool to administer assessments to students.
c. Utilizing technology as a tool for communication among stakeholders.
d. Utilizing technology as a tool to collect, organize, and analyze data for school improvement and progress monitoring.

40. Experts find that, to build community capacity for contributing to school improvement, school leaders and staff must transcend traditional activities. What is true about how they can further continue community collaboration for school improvement?

a. For productive partnerships, schools should give stakeholders information only as they request it.
b. School leaders and staff should identify which community members can participate meaningfully.
c. All collaborations with community members should align directly with the campus vision and goals.
d. To engage and retain community partners, schools should limit the achievement data they share.

41. Transformational school leadership has been found in research as most effective for modeling and encouraging staff development and self-improvement. Which of the following best represents the strategies of transformational school leaders?

a. They build school structures to encourage staff decision-making participation.
b. They take responsibility for everything rather than delegating duties or tasks.
c. They give teachers ample direction for making decisions instead of autonomy.
d. They take charge of determining school priorities to unite dissenting teachers.

42. Alternative high school principals Mohr and Dichter (2001) codified developmental stages that school staff undergo to become learning communities. Which stage is associated with the emergence of a sense of community?

a. The stage involving conflict.
b. The honeymoon stage.
c. The confusion stage.
d. The mature stage.

43. Which of the following strategies most accurately identifies the school leader's role in implementing professional development?

a. Staff development is the sole responsibility of the school leader.
b. A school leader should delegate the implementation of professional development to the administrative team.
c. A school leader should leverage teacher leaders in the implementation of professional development.
d. School leaders are directly responsible for implementing professional development but should utilize their administrative team and teacher leaders where appropriate.

44. What have researchers found regarding the relationship between student academic self-concepts and student outcomes?

a. Students' academic self-concepts are correlated with their succeeding later in life.
b. Students' academic self-concepts are correlated with their academic achievement.
c. Students' academic self-concepts are correlated with socioeconomic status more than home settings.
d. Students' academic self-concepts are correlated with enrollment in smaller schools.

45. When schools and leaders implement the continuous school improvement process, which should they do *first*?

a. Establish specific goals for school improvements.
b. Reflect on instructional and leadership practices.
c. Implement strategies for specific improvements.
d. Conduct needs assessments for their schools.

46. Which of the following is most used in self-assessment to facilitate professional development?

a. Teachers write in journals about their work.
b. Teachers apply advice they receive to work.
c. Teachers analyze videos of their instruction.
d. Teachers benefit from others' experiences.

47. Which of these is a valid guideline for school leaders to support staff throughout their professional development (PD)?

a. To be job-embedded and school-based, PD must occur in the school building.
b. For effective PD, teachers must not learn passively, but be actively involved.
c. Because teachers are the ones involved in PD, it should be teacher-centered.
d. PD must be done independently to ensure individual learning and growth.

48. Of the following, which accurately reflects a principle of adult learning that applies to professional development (PD) for teachers?

a. Adults learn best when participation in PD is required.
b. Adults learn best when learning materials are selected and provided.
c. Adults learn best when they are involved in planning the instruction.
d. Adults learn best when informed about how they will be assessed prior to participation.

49. Which of the following most correctly represents criteria requiring a school to hold a Manifestation Determination Review for a student who receives special education services?

a. The school seeks a discipline-related placement change for more than 10 days in a row.
b. The school suspends a student on a one-time basis for more than 10 consecutive days.
c. The school suspends a student for 10 or more days in a school year for any reason.
d. The school creates or revises a behavior intervention plan.

50. With the exception of some, many public-school districts receive the largest proportion of funding from which of the following sources?

a. Federal government.
b. Their city government.
c. The state government.
d. Various other sources.

51. To evaluate teacher effectiveness in applying instructional strategies, school leaders need a working knowledge of student-centered, research-based teaching methods. What is most true about these?

a. The Socratic method is a useful, research-based strategy for delivering instruction.
b. Project-based learning requires technology integration in order to be implemented effectively.
c. Cooperative learning has been proven to be an effective, research-based instructional strategy.
d. It is necessary for teachers to utilize technology to deliver instruction in order to be effective.

52. Which of the following is the best example a school leader utilizing technology to support effective school organization management?

a. Using technology to reconcile the budget and coordinate facility operations.
b. Using technology to text message and email stakeholders about meetings.
c. Using technology to collect, disaggregate, and analyze different school data.
d. Using technology to facilitate multiple stakeholder contributions to projects.

53. According to multiple research studies, what is a characteristic of school leaders related to evaluating teacher effectiveness?

a. The most effective school leaders are better at identifying the best candidates for hiring as teachers.
b. The most effective school leaders are better at identifying the best and worst teachers on their staff.
c. The most effective teachers are attracted to the schools whose leaders have hired the best teachers.
d. The most effective school leaders are better at identifying better and average teachers than poorer ones.

54. How can a school and its leaders best control the quality of the teaching faculty?

a. Focus on retaining effective teachers to prevent having to recruit new teachers.
b. Focus on attracting, retaining, and developing effective teachers.
c. Focus on hiring and developing effective teachers rather than recruiting new teachers.
d. Focus on retaining quality teachers rather than firing ineffective teachers.

55. Which of the following is the best description of a transactional leader?

a. Willing to purchase new equipment to improve the current system.
b. Works to change the culture by implementing new policies.
c. Pursues efficiency in the school system through strong supervision.
d. Seeks staff and community involvement in developing new ideas.

56. According to the federal government, the core components of a response strategy to information system threats and breaches are policy, plan, and procedure. Which of the following is a function of the policy component?

a. Defining staff responsibilities and mechanisms for remediation.
b. Identifying needed management support and school resources.
c. Standardizing response tasks and behaviors and averting errors.
d. Conducting risk assessments on a regular basis as a preparation.

57. What do psychologists recommend regarding tiered models of student behavior management in education?

a. Tiered models of behavior management work only with school-wide behavior support systems.
b. Tiered models of behavior management are most effective when addressing individual disruptive student behavior.
c. Tiered models of behavior management are most applicable for classroom or school-wide implementation.
d. Tiered models of behavior management are judged best for individuals, classrooms, or schools.

58. Which of the following criteria would make a school the best candidate for implementing an integrated management system as new technology for managing school operations?

a. The school has not been using any digital management system.
b. The school has been using one management system with no plans for more.
c. The school has one or more systems and plans on adding more systems.
d. The school wants separate system policies and documentation.

59. Which of the following is most effective in motivating members of the educational community when implementing new policies?

a. Delegating authority to staff members.
b. Communicating unexpected barriers to the community as they arise.
c. Sharing the policies frequently using a variety of communication channels.
d. Including stakeholders in the development of new policies.

60. Who typically makes student enrollment projections for determining school budgets?

a. District Offices of Achievement and Accountability alone project the student enrollments.
b. District Offices of Achievement and Accountability with school leader revision as needed.
c. The school leader alone projects the student enrollments for his or her school every year.
d. Final projections are by committees from the district finance and student support offices.

61. Which of the following describes the school district policy to allow principals autonomy to spend their campus budget as they see fit?

a. Local school management.
b. Hybrid financial decision-making.
c. Budgetary autonomy.
d. Decentralization.

62. Which of these is true about the relationship between federal, state, and local laws, and local policies as is relates to the school leader's responsibilities?

a. The school leader must interpret federal and state laws to determine how these apply at the campus level.
b. The school leader is responsible for influencing policies and laws at all levels.
c. The school leader must adhere to local policies unless they directly conflict with state or federal law.
d. The school leader must vote for federal, state, and local laws in accordance with school district policy.

63. What correctly represents National Education Association (NEA) guidelines for school acceptable use policies (AUPs) regarding classroom Internet technology?

a. It should have a policy statement including covered computer services and student use conditions.
b. It should have a definition section covering important terms used, but a preamble is not necessary.
c. It should include a section that defines acceptable use, but not one that defines unacceptable use.
d. It should include a violations or sanctions section, which should only define violations of the policy.

64. The majority of US state laws designate which school professionals as mandated reporters of child abuse and neglect?

a. Healthcare and mental health professionals, but not childcare providers.
b. Teachers, principals, and other school personnel are required to report.
c. Social workers instead of school social workers are mandated reporters.
d. Law enforcement officers, but not medical examiners and coroners.

65. Which of the following best describes school leader responsibilities related to school safety policies?

a. Leaders must ensure school safety policies comply with federal laws only.
b. Leaders must notify staff and parents in advance of any changes affecting safety or health.
c. Leaders are solely responsible for developing and revising safety policies.
d. Leaders do not have the responsibility of warning parents about environmental hazards.

66. School emergency response team organization is modeled after the Incident Command System (ICS) of Homeland Security's National Incident Management System (NIMS). Main ICS functions include Finance. Which of the ICS Management Systems identifies services and resources to support incident response needs?

a. Logistics.
b. Planning.
c. Command.
d. Operations.

67. Which is a practice that national research studies find school leaders should *avoid* when speaking publicly and in other communication with key stakeholders?

a. Taking advantage of the political environment.
b. Using commonly understood language with most audiences.
c. Communicating in response to sensitive situations.
d. Becoming engaged in large scale open forums.

68. Which of the following is the least effective way that school leaders can create inclusive school communities?

a. Encourage students whose parents do not speak English to translate for them when interacting with school staff.
b. Provide video recordings and resources to parents who miss workshops and meetings.
c. Validate, honor, and thank family and community for supporting the school.
d. Hire parent liaisons to help parents access resources and services offered by the school.

69. What must school leaders consider to mobilize and develop community school support?

a. Businesses and community-based organizations use the same language that educators use.
b. Exchanging and matching visions, missions, wants, and needs with stakeholders is sufficient.
c. Prospective community partners primarily want to know how collaboration benefits schools.
d. Prospective partner motivations are as varied as the organizations interested in partnership.

70. Which of the following is true about proactive strategies that successful school leaders have used to overcome resistance to change by school staff, families, communities, and school districts?

a. People fear change irrespective of school leader commitment.
b. Administrative support networks enhance change acceptance.
c. Establishing priorities tends to strengthen resistance to change.
d. How school leaders communicate has no impact on resistance.

71. Which of the following sources of data would be most beneficial for a school leader to analyze prior to developing or revising the school vision and goals?

a. Teacher turnover data, failure rates, and satisfaction survey results.
b. Student performance data, student attendance data, and student promotion rates.
c. Community engagement rates.
d. School accountability ratings for the last three years.

72. A school leader has developed the vision and goals in collaboration with the campus leadership team and community stakeholders. Which of the following is the best step that the school leader should take next?

a. Develop a strategic plan for implementing the vision and goals.
b. Host a community meeting to present the vision and goals to all stakeholders.
c. Delegate tasks to leadership team members to implement the vision and goals.
d. Host a meeting with campus staff to present the vision and goals and inform them of their duties and responsibilities related to the vision and goals.

73. A school principal would like to engage a variety of stakeholders to inform the development of the school mission and vision. Which of the following strategies would best accomplish this goal?

a. Host a school assembly to get feedback from the student body.
b. Distribute a survey to students, parents, staff, and community members.
c. Create a committee of teacher, students, and parents.
d. Meet with local business owners in the community.

74. The school leader has established the school goals for the school year and is developing a plan for assessing and monitoring progress. Which of the following strategies would be most effective for monitoring goal progress?

a. Require leadership team members who have been delegated tasks to report on what they have accomplished each week.
b. Review student academic performance data in preparation for quarterly community meetings.
c. Establish time intervals for reviewing indicators of performance, such as monthly or according to grading periods.
d. Purchase and implement an electronic data management platform that sends automatic notifications when data does not meet predetermined thresholds.

75. A new middle school principal is concerned about the academic performance of seventh grade students in math. Which of the following actions should the principal take first when developing a plan to improve students' math scores?

a. Identify the curriculum, resources, and instructional strategies currently in use.
b. Allocate funding for math tutors.
c. Reassign struggling students to stronger teachers.
d. Administer additional math assessments to identify student weaknesses in math.

76. A math intervention program that was implemented on a high school campus for the previous school year was funded by a grant that is expired. The principal must determine whether to fund the program using the local budget or to eliminate the program. Which of the following data points would best inform the principal as to whether the math intervention program should continue to be funded?

a. Student attendance in the program.
b. Feedback from students regarding the program.
c. Student math performance data from the beginning of the school year compared to the end of the school year.
d. Student performance on the state mandated assessment for the previous school year.

77. The Campus Technology Coordinator recommends to the principal that new desktop computers be purchased for three of the campus's computer labs. The Dean of Instruction recommends that classroom technology should be upgraded first. Which of the following strategies should the principal implement first to decide how to prioritize these recommendations in the school's technology budget?

a. The principal should physically inspect the current equipment to determine which is in the most need of replacement.
b. The principal should refer to the campus improvement plan to determine how the recommendations align with the vision and goals for the school.
c. The principal should seek donations from stakeholders to assist with improving technology across the campus.
d. The principal should determine which of the recommendations is most economical.

78. Which of the following professional development activities would likely have the most impact on current teacher performance?

a. A self-paced book study program for all teachers.
b. Online courses that teachers select and participate in individually at their own pace.
c. A four-hour in-person training conducted during the school year.
d. A hybrid online and in-person six-week course that meets weekly for a cohort of teachers.

79. During the annual summer meeting, the math department chair expresses concern that the math teachers do not have enough collaborative time to plan lessons and discuss student performance. Which of the following solutions would best address the department chair's concern?

a. Make adjustments to the master schedule to allot collaborative planning time for the math department.
b. Offer extra duty pay for math teachers to stay after school and plan together.
c. Purchase a technology platform that will allow the teachers to communicate asynchronously online.
d. Place substitute teachers in the math classrooms monthly to allow teachers time to plan together.

80. Which of the following practices by school leaders most effectively improves teacher practice and student learning?

a. Reviewing student performance data and sharing aggregated results with teachers.
b. Administering self-assessment surveys to teachers.
c. Conducting regular classroom observations and providing timely feedback.
d. Offering educational resources to teachers related to their identified areas of weakness.

81. The Dean of Instruction conducted a classroom observation of a 7th grade math teacher and noticed that the math teacher was not following the curriculum for the math department. When asked, the math teacher informed the dean that the students were not ready for the standards identified in the curriculum and that he chose to review standards from 6th grade instead.

Which of the following would be the best response from the dean to the math teacher?

a. Commend the math teacher for addressing the gaps in student learning.
b. Require that the math teacher attend training on the math curriculum.
c. Model instruction of the standards outlined in the curriculum.
d. Direct the math teacher to teach the standards outlined in the curriculum.

82. Which of the following actions best demonstrates collaboration with teachers to maintain an instructional program that delivers standards-based instruction?

a. Audit instructional materials used in the classroom, including worksheets and teacher-developed materials.
b. Compare student course grades to performance on standardized tests.
c. Engage in professional learning communities with teachers to contribute to planning discussions about the curriculum.
d. Survey teachers to obtain feedback about new curriculum options.

83. A school leader wants to become more involved in analyzing student work on campus. Which of the following actions should the school leader take to accomplish this goal?

a. Audit student work samples and discuss the student performance demonstrated with the teachers who assigned the work.
b. Monitor teacher grade books.
c. Host a science fair.
d. Mandate that teachers assess student learning using portfolios.

84. A Dean of Instruction of a middle school wants to increase the number and variety of resources that teachers have access to. Which of the following actions should the dean take to accomplish this goal?

a. Encourage teachers to purchase instructional resources and provide reimbursement for their expenses.
b. Survey teachers to identify which resources they would like to have and purchase resources from their suggestions.
c. Provide teachers with asynchronous, on-demand professional development sessions online.
d. Seek free and discounted resources from vendors in the local area.

85. Which of the following actions best demonstrates a middle school leader monitoring instructional practices and student progress to ensure that all students are prepared for a challenging curriculum?

a. Offering a summer bridge program for underperforming seventh grade students entering eighth grade.
b. Reviewing the performance of incoming sixth grade students on standardized tests.
c. Evaluating the course grades of eighth grade students enrolled in an Algebra I course for high school credit.
d. Comparing student performance on standardized tests to course grades to determine alignment of assessment.

86. A high school principal is concerned that ninth grade students who read below grade level are not performing well on benchmark tests in Reading and Writing. Which of the following steps should the principal take to best address this concern?

a. Provide test preparation sessions for these students after school and on weekends and monitor student attendance to the sessions.
b. Integrate reading and writing skills into all subject areas and provide training to all teachers on fundamental reading strategies.
c. Increase the opportunities that students have to spend in the school library.
d. Purchase a reading software program that students can use at home.

87. The school principal reviews classroom observation and feedback with assistant principals weekly, but often has very few classroom observations of their own conducted in preparation for the weekly meeting. What action should the school principal take to increase the frequency of classroom visits?

a. Make a commitment to visit classrooms every morning before the day gets too busy.
b. Clear their schedule on a specific day of the week to dedicate to classroom visits.
c. Plan out the classrooms that should be visited for the week and add them to the calendar with reminders.
d. Carry classroom observation forms at all times and visit classrooms when an opportunity presents itself.

88. A middle school principal wants to improve the quality of teaching and learning on campus on a continuous basis throughout the school year rather than only reviewing annual performance data and making changes prior to the start of the school year. Which of the following strategies would best help the principal to achieve this goal?

a. Assess students every six weeks using benchmark exams and use the data to adjust the instructional program.
b. At the start of the school year, administer a comprehensive exam to determine what information students retained over the summer.
c. Administer a comprehensive exam to students at the beginning of the school year, in the middle of the school year, and at the end of the school year and use the data to make plans for the following school year.
d. Require that teachers maintain portfolios for all students to demonstrate learning and growth over the course of the school year.

89. A high school principal has been invited by a community leader to participate in a community event in which the principal will have a brief opportunity to address the community. Of the following, which information would be most important to share with the community stakeholders at this event?

a. Provide information on how to sign up to be a volunteer at the school.
b. Recruit volunteers and mentors for at-risk students.
c. Provide updates on progress toward the school vision and goals.
d. Describe opportunities to collaborate with businesses in the community.

90. Which of the following best demonstrates that the school leader ensures that the physical plant is functional and in compliance with local, state, and federal regulations?

a. The school leader includes the Plant Operator in leadership meetings to report on the status of the school facility.
b. The school leader requires that teachers and staff submit monthly reports regarding the condition of their work areas, such as classrooms and offices.
c. The school leader maintains hard and soft copies of documents necessary for audits by local agencies.
d. The school leader physically inspects the school facility weekly.

91. For the third subsequent year, a school leader has had 40 percent turnover of teaching staff. This high rate of turnover has impacted the campus negatively and the school leader wants to address this concern. In a stakeholder meeting, the leader asks members to brainstorm suggestions for addressing teacher retention. Which of the following suggestions should the school leader implement first?

a. Administer a survey to teachers to get their feedback on what they like and dislike about working at the campus.
b. Petition the district to raise teacher salaries.
c. Offer bonuses to teachers who produce good student performance results on standardized assessments.
d. Provide mentors to new teachers on campus.

92. Which of the following does not demonstrate that an education leader proactively addresses challenges to student emotional safety?

a. The education leader collaborates with the school counselor to design a referral system for students experiencing an emotional or mental crisis.
b. The education leader provides information about free resources in the community for mental health needs to all parents and stakeholders at the beginning of the school year.
c. The education leader creates a grief counseling group following the suicide of a student.
d. The education leader schedules a counselor to visit the school monthly.

93. An elementary school principal serves at a school in which many of the parents of students speak little or no English. The language barrier creates challenges in communication, parent engagement, and the reinforcement of learning at home. Which of the following actions would best help the principal to address this challenge?

a. Hire a translator to communicate with parents.
b. Partner with an adult ESL program in the community and offer free ESL classes on campus.
c. Translate all school documents to the languages of the parents.
d. Ask students to translate information for their parents.

94. The school principal was informed by school district personnel that a parent complaint had been filed against the school. A student's relative who did not have guardianship of the student called the school and was informed by the attendance clerk of the student's schedule and attendance. Which of the following best describes the error of the principal?

a. The principal failed to monitor the systems and procedures to protect the confidentiality of the student.
b. The principal had poor judgment in hiring the attendance clerk.
c. The principal should have taken the phone call themselves.
d. The principal did not make an error in this situation.

95. A high school principal determines that it is no longer financially viable to sponsor the fine arts program at the school. Enrollment in fine arts courses has steadily decreased over the past four school years and the expenses of the program have exceed the budget. However, the principal knows that many stakeholders in the community feel strongly about having a fine arts program. Which of the following represents the best action for the school principal?

a. Continue to offer the fine arts program.
b. Make an announcement to the students and staff that there will not be a fine arts program next year.
c. Host a fundraiser for the fine arts program.
d. Host a meeting to explain to stakeholders the reasons for eliminating the fine arts program.

96. A teacher sponsors an afterschool club for knitting. Members of the club are all female students, but a male student has requested to participate. The sponsor told the student he could not participate because knitting was an activity for girls. The male student and his parents complained to the principal. Which of the following actions should the principal take first?

a. Create a knitting club for male students.
b. Force the sponsor to allow the male student to participate.
c. Speak with the teacher about the stereotypes and bias that impacted their decision.
d. Support the sponsor's decision because it is their club.

97. A school principal would like to develop a positive partnership with the school community. Which of the following actions would best help the principal to achieve this goal?

a. Publish a monthly school newsletter with reminders for important school events.
b. Host a student award ceremony each semester to highlight school and student successes.
c. Attend all school athletic events.
d. Send a survey to all community members to get their feedback on school performance.

98. A doctor who has a clinic in the community informs the principal that she is willing to provide free physicals to students at the school who would like to participate in athletics. How should the principal respond?

a. Decline the offer because students are responsible for getting physicals completed on their own.
b. Decline the offer if all students cannot receive a physical, not just athletes.
c. Accept the offer and create a log to document students who take advantage of the free physical.
d. Accept the offer only if the doctor can complete the physicals on campus after school hours.

99. At a PTA meeting, a concerned community member stated that there were no programs offered at the high school that prepared students for jobs in the community and that there was too much focus on sending students to college. Which of the following best describes the action that the principal can take to address the community member's concern?

a. Inform the community member that preparing students for college is the school's primary responsibility.
b. Promise the community member that course offerings will be revised for the upcoming school year.
c. Ask the community member which jobs in the community the school should prepare students for.
d. Collect and review employment trend data in the community to determine if school course offerings need to be revised to meet community needs.

100. The Dean of Instruction analyzed data from the most recent benchmark assessment and noticed that when the data was disaggregated by race and ethnicity, a particular group failed to meet performance standards. How should the dean address this?

a. Talk to teachers who instruct the demographic group and students that belong to the demographic group to identify the challenges they are facing in mastering the content.
b. Contact the parents of the students who were not successful and inform them that their child needs tutoring.
c. Observe the teachers who instruct the demographic group to determine their efficacy.
d. Develop a schedule of tutorials and remediation for the students who did not master the content.

Constructed Response

1. As the school leader, you have selected a leadership team to assist with leading the school program. Your leadership team is composed of a Dean of Instruction, two assistant principals, and a Dean of Students. Individual team members are capable of performing their job; however, the leadership team does not work well with one another. Their inability to coordinate their efforts and collaborate has led to ineffective leadership on campus and conflicting initiatives.

Write an approximately 150-300-word address to your leadership team. Include the following:

- Identify the effects of the leadership team's behavior on the campus.
- Explain how a campus leadership team should function.
- Identify at least one step you will take as school leader to address this issue.

2. You are the principal of a large high school that enrolls students from three large middle schools in the school district. Over the last two years, data has shown that students from one of the middle schools are disproportionately identified as receiving special education services when compared to the students matriculating from the other two middle schools. This has led to a significant increase in the number of students receiving special education services on your campus. Currently there is a shortage of special education teachers and classroom teachers have limited knowledge of differentiating instruction. Write an approximately 150-300-word address to classroom teachers, special educators, and school leaders about your intention to explore solutions for better meeting special student needs. Include the following:

- Describe one major issue you need to consider in identifying, planning, and implementing solutions for meeting special student needs.
- Explain what impacts the issue you described will have on your school's capacity for achieving the goal of improving learning and performance for students with special needs.
- Specify one kind of information or data that would especially inform your process of exploring, finding, and applying effective solutions for classroom teachers, special educators, and others to meet special student needs.
- Explain why and how the information or data you specified would inform this process.

3. As school principal, you have been informed by your district office that, in the next school year, community growth will result in a significant increase in student enrollment at your school. At the same time, funding allocations for many programs such as technology, fine arts, and athletics have been reduced. In planning the school budget for the coming fiscal year, you want the input and collaboration of school staff. You convene a meeting of members representing the faculty, staff, office, food service, transportation, and other departments. Write an approximately 150-300-word document to prepare all meeting attendees for discussion, brainstorming, and planning. Include the following:

- Give a description of one issue you find central to addressing the fulfillment of the most important school programs and services in view of the exigencies of increased enrollment and decreased finances.
- Identify at least one step the school could take to save on expenses while still offering students needed programs and services.
- Explain how this step would help to resolve the coming challenge.

Answer Key and Explanations for Test #1

Multiple Choice Questions

1. C: School leaders and others should analyze school data based upon formative classroom assessments and standardized state summative assessments. The data analyzed should include data across grade levels, across school years, by subjects, by student cohorts, by student special populations, and by individual teachers, when possible. Analysis of data should be holistic in order to identify school strengths, needs for improvement, and trends to properly inform the school vision and mission.

2. B: Schools and school leaders use data they have collected for setting goals aligned with their school vision and mission. Data-based decision-making is a best practice for school leaders. Data should be collected for all decision making and data can be collected in the forms of quantitative data, such as standardized assessment results, attendance rates, etc., or qualitative data such as survey feedback. School goals must be aligned with the school vision and mission so that progress toward established goals is connected to achieving the school vision and mission.

3. D: When school visions are developed through collaboration among employees, they tend to be more appropriate to the contexts of their local school districts, which is an advantage. Collaboratively developed school visions typically are *not* implemented as quickly as those personally developed by school leaders, which also tend to be clearer and more coherent than those developed collaboratively. Collaboratively developed school visions do take longer to develop, slowing change, which is a disadvantage, not an advantage.

4. A: In some states, teachers do not have to be fully certified to teach in a public school. Teachers who are new to the profession and may be enrolled in an alternative teacher certification program may be allowed to teach in a public school on a probationary status. However, all teachers must demonstrate subject-matter competency prior to being deemed highly qualified and able to teach in a public school. States may vary in their requirements for teacher certification; therefore, a teacher who is highly qualified in one state may have to meet additional qualifications if they move to another state.

5. C: All levels, from individual schools to state education departments, must ultimately align with federal policy to make major educational goals match the national vision. However, within this hierarchy, specific expressions of policy, e.g., standardized test instruments, reflect the next higher level. Thus, state standardized tests reflect federal standards, not just state standards; individual schools *directly* apply standards from their school systems, not state standards, which in turn reflect the standards of their school districts, which in turn *directly* apply state standards, not federal standards.

6. B: To foster equity and inclusion in education, school leaders should assure all their teachers develop curriculum and differentiated instruction that are *both* developmentally appropriate *and* culturally diverse; model respect for diversity in their own behaviors, and offer their schools and communities multiple ways for celebrating diversity; involve suitable culturally diverse community stakeholders in school decisions, which *is* their job; and hold all members of their school communities accountable for valuing diversity, equity, and inclusion, not just themselves.

7. C: Distributive leadership is a leadership style that shares leadership roles and responsibilities with others in a deliberate and systematic way. Providing team members with leadership opportunities builds capacity and helps to cultivate team members into leaders. Practicing distributive leadership also helps to foster change and improvement because the ideas and talent of team members are leveraged and utilized.

8. A: Research studies find that, for implementing school-wide technology adoption, required factors are sufficient resources and support, professional development, school structure, school organization, and leadership. Effective professional development must be intentionally and carefully planned, designed with goals in mind, provided continually to keep up with constant changes in the teaching profession, and integrated system-wide or school-wide as part of the school culture through teacher collaboration and sharing of knowledge.

9. D: The National Education Association (NEA) Code of Ethics principle of Commitment to the Student prohibits *unreasonably preventing* students from independently pursuing learning and *unreasonably denying* student access to various perspectives, not encouraging these. It *requires*, not prohibits, reasonable efforts to safeguard students against harm to health, safety, or learning. It prohibits *suppressing*, not disclosing, any information pertinent to student progress. However, it does prohibit disclosing student information when not legally or professionally required.

10. A: State funding under Title I and Smart Start legislation is often available as a way for school leaders to hire school parent facilitators, whose jobs are to involve families in their children's educations. School leaders should not always expect for parents to visit the school. Instead, school leaders should also be visible in the community to facilitate family involvement. School leaders can develop community relationships by beginning with parents who are already involved, but make an effort to involve parents who have not been previously involved. Fostering parental involvement requires two-way communication, not just one-way communication such as robocalls or newsletters.

11. C: Group consensus is an ideal approach for collaborative decisions in that all participants' voices are heard, and every member must provide input and agree with the group decision. However, it is more time-consuming, not more time-efficient, than majority rule or committee decision-making. Majority rule is the method wherein minority voters' commitment can be undermined. Committee decision-making is the method whereby committee members may feel their time and effort were wasted if members of the larger group frequently override committee decisions.

12. B: Among resource limitations, inadequate school counselor-to-student ratios are attributable to funding and budget cuts, not accountability mandates. Inadequate in-service development for new support staff is attributable to various factors, including cultural influences stigmatizing mental health issues, lowering their priority in schools; leadership and organizational deficits; and funding deficits, ineffective resource allocation, etc.—not accountability mandates. Inadequate school district mental health budgeting is not federally mandated for accountability. Federal accountability requirements have changed school counselor responsibilities from addressing student mental health to addressing student academic achievement, reducing professional support services.

13. A: Traditionally, bus drivers are considered school support staff, typically under the district Transportation Department. They serve multiple school locations and are usually supervised by an employee in the Transportation Department. Custodians and cafeteria workers are often dedicated to one campus and may be supervised by the campus principal. Volunteers are unpaid and not officially school district employees, but are supervised by the campus principal to ensure compliance with policies and procedures. However, school districts may have differing organizational polices and supervision of campus personnel.

14. D: Focused discussions and effective interaction between students are indicators that the instructional activities are effective. Student discourse, whether teacher-facilitated or independent, is an indicator or learning and mastery of content. Increased student attendance is a positive student outcome but is not necessarily the direct result of a particular instructional activity. Differentiated instruction and flexible student grouping are instructional strategies, not outcomes.

15. A: Prior to adopting curriculum, the alignment of the curriculum to learning standards must be verified. Curriculum that is not aligned will not be effective in instruction students and ensuring their performance on state-mandated assessments. After the alignment has been verified, the curriculum may be vetted by various stakeholders and approved for use by the school board.

16. D: School leaders should not assign teachers to write technology standards. Integrating technology does help students meet curriculum standards. School leaders and faculty should require students to master any existing technology standards as cross-curricular and procedural knowledge and skills. Experts advise school leaders and teachers to focus not on learning about technology, but on learning with technology.

17. B: To provide teachers with effective feedback and collaboration, school leaders must know that student motivation and learning are influenced by different types of assessments; that despite "objective" tests, machine scoring, etc., ultimately assessment is based in the judgment, assumptions, and values of professional educators who design, score, interpret, and grade assessments; that not only is error inevitable in all assessment, but moreover it is typically underestimated; and that reliability in assessment involves scores and results, *not* tests or instruments.

18. D: Leaders can encourage self-direction in improving among faculty and staff by modeling this behavior. Leaders who are transparent about their own areas of improvement will encourage and set an example for employees. Additionally, the school leader should actively engage employees in self-assessment as well as make resources available for doing so. However, a leader should not leave self-improvement up to employees as it will likely not be done. Employees need support, resources, and encouragement to engage in self-directed improvement.

19. C: Each of the options represents a supportive way of promoting professional development, but choice C is primarily an individual activity and not a way of building up a collaborative learning environment among professionals. Action research is the process of doing informal studies in the school environment to try to find improved practices. While the research is often done alone, the intent of action research is to share with other members of the learning community, making it a collaborative effort in most cases. Professional learning communities (PLCs) are teams of educators who work together to identify concerns and meet needs together and is an excellent way for teachers to improve their skills through professional collaboration. Structured observations are usually something the school administration takes on to ensure a quality control on teaching, but even though it often is top-down oriented, the process is inherently collaborative in that one professional comes and observes another teacher and provides specific feedback to help improve professional practices.

20. C: Study questions at the ends of textbook chapters typically help students recall or identify, locate, interpret, and apply information they just read more than reflect. Graphic organizers help students visualize and organize verbal, numerical, and abstract information. Worksheets help students practice what they have just learned. Writing regularly in journals promotes and gives students a method for reflection.

21. C: Prior to the integration of technology into instructional practice, it was difficult for teachers to individualize instruction for students as it relates to content and pace. Technology applications allow teachers to facilitate instruction that meets the students' individual needs and allows students to work at their own pace toward mastery. Heterogenous student grouping can be a beneficial strategy but is not directly related to technology use in the classroom. Similarly, passive and active learning can occur with or without technology integration. Project-based learning can be facilitated with technology, but it is not a requirement.

22. D: The least restrictive environment for a student who receives special education services is the same environment as their peers who do not receive these services. Any time a student is removed from the main program of education, their environment is restricted. A students LRE is determined by their Individualized Education Plan and may differ based on their learning needs. However, a student's IEP and academic performance must be reviewed regularly to ensure that the student is in the least restrictive environment possible.

23. A: Tiered positive behavior support models have been found highly effective as school-wide classroom management systems because they incorporate not only prevention of behavior problems before they occur, but also interventions for existing or developing behavior problems. Also, by reducing the incidence of problem behaviors, these models provide *more* time for students to be engaged academically.

24. A: A supportive school climate occurs when students have resources readily available to them that can help them feel supported and to overcome challenges that they may face. The resources available should be based on student needs, such as counseling, mentorship, social activities, and others. A supportive school climate should foster peer relationships among peers intentionally rather than allowing them to happen by chance because students share common schedules. While policy handbooks for students are useful, they do not directly contribute to a supportive school environment. On the other hand, student interactions with adults on campus can directly impact students' feelings of being supported.

25. B: Instruction can be differentiated based on content, process, or product. Differentiating instruction based on product means that the teacher provides multiple ways for a student to demonstrate mastery. Allowing students to write an essay gives students an opportunity to demonstrate mastery in written form or in spoken form. Providing students with different versions of assessments is still assessing students using a test and does not constitute differentiated instruction.

26. B: Professional Learning Committees (PLC) are designed to facilitate collaboration among teachers based on grade levels, subject area, or other commonalities. In PLCs, educators use quantitative and qualitative data to make decisions about students and are guided by the following questions: What do we want students to learn? What do we do if they do not learn it? What do we do if they learn it? Communicating with parents and submitting reports often include sharing of data, but do not necessarily indicate that the data is used to make decisions. Requiring teachers to host tutorial sessions for students is a beneficial intervention, but may not be a directive based on data.

27. D: School system guidelines recommend that, in giving teachers observational feedback, school leaders should focus feedback discussions by developing open-ended questions that target specific areas for each teacher, explicitly name two or three teacher strengths they observed, identify one area for improvement that will make the most impact on student learning and teacher development, and develop a few specific and attainable next steps for each teacher to take. Effective observational feedback should include strengths and weaknesses and recommendations for next steps should be clear and attainable.

28. C: A successful new teacher induction program will provide opportunities for new teachers to collaborate with one another and with more experienced teachers. Additionally, a successful program will incorporate leadership development opportunities for new teachers to explore and refine their leadership skills. New teachers should receive strategic professional coaching and be assigned a mentor based on experience and effectiveness of the mentoring staff member. While the school leader is responsible for ensuring that an effective induction program in place, there are other instructional staff and campus leaders who can add value to the induction program by facilitating various aspects of the program.

29. C: School principals should look for evidence of learning when conducting a classroom observation. Students should be given opportunities to respond and demonstrate learning throughout the lesson so that the teacher and the observer can determine whether students are learning the content. These opportunities may occur as questioning strategies, discussion, or through guided and independent practice. It is important for teachers to be comfortable with the instructional content and method of delivery, but this is not a primary focus of a classroom observation as a novice teacher can be nervous yet still effective. Additionally, the physical classroom setup should be conducive to learning but is not the primary focus of a classroom observation.

30. A: Research studies have found the most effective implementations of school data use initiatives were most proactive, offering regular and expert system data use training of school leaders, leadership skills advice and coaching, and vigorous promotion. These got significantly better results even comparing districts using similar data systems, showing implementation was more important than the data system. Researchers observed that, although technology is necessary to support data initiatives, it alone is not the answer to school data use. Studies also found teams use data technology systems more quickly and productively than individual teachers.

31. B: Testing accommodations for some students based on their individual needs are not unfair, but actually make assessments fairer and also more valid. School leaders can help decrease achievement gaps among student cultural groups and backgrounds by using student data to monitor progress regularly. However, extensive testing of students, especially to the impediment of instruction, can be detrimental to students who are already low performing. Data collected from assessments, even non-standardized formative assessments, can be used to monitor student progress and inform instructional decisions.

32. A: The US Departments of Education's and Justice's school discipline guidance package intends to lower significant overall annual student expulsion and suspension rates, including disproportionate overrepresentation of students with disabilities and from other minorities. The package also aims to help schools establish positive learning environments *and* enhance school safety; to aid schools having difficulty establishing safe, positive learning environments, even though violent school incidents overall are less than before; and to ensure school behavioral interventions are both federally legal *and* non-discriminatory.

33. B: School leaders can promote equitable access to curriculum for all students and parents by making staff more comfortable discussing diversity issues, social justice, and values, which will promote equity; clarifying staff misconceptions related to deficit theories about minorities and diverse groups; modeling equity beliefs and behaviors in daily interactions; confronting discrimination and stereotyping in actions and language; creating safe school environments where all students feel welcomed and valued; and establishing support networks for students harassed over cultural, sexual, and/or gender identity.

34. B: School improvement plans have been found to increase parental meeting and student school attendance; student enrollment and achievement; parental involvement in policies, procedures, advocacy, organizing, and events; and to decrease student behavior problems while increasing student achievement. School system leaders have also established central office policies and structures that increased parental engagement, not only in individual schools but also system-wide.

35. A: In many American communities and states, schools provide the chief—and often the only—mental health (MH) services that children receive. Parents are more comfortable with such services when they are provided in familiar school settings by familiar staff, rather than avoiding them. Research studies find students are *more* likely to seek counseling services in schools than to look elsewhere. Another reason for school-community collaboration is the necessity of coordinating school and community MH services, not separating them.

36. C: In school change processes, first-order changes represent specific strategies for implementing deeper changes in educational ideas and philosophies. Thus, forming a different instructional approach is a second-order change, as are forming new interactions and relationships and forming a sense of collaborative ownership among educational stakeholders. For implementing that sense of shared ownership, forming site-based school advisory councils is an example of a corresponding first-order change.

37. A: The Supportive School Discipline Initiative (SSDI) included guidance for positive school discipline practices to keep students in school by providing alternatives to exclusionary methods like suspension and expulsion. This guidance was produced jointly by the US Departments of Education and Justice to ensure enforcement of federal civil rights protections against discrimination. It provides school resources with helpful information rather than getting it from them. The SSDI's purpose was to keep student discipline from escalating to the police or prison systems, not to continue this trend.

38. D: In SPBS programs, tier 3 is for the small proportion of students not responding to tier 1 or tier 2 interventions. It involves intensive, individualized interventions tailored to each student. Small socio-emotional group instruction in social and emotional skills, daily student check-in and check-out procedures, and enlisting family support for small-group intervention and instruction are all techniques associated with tier 2.

39. D: A primary aspect of implementing a school improvement plan is to use data to assess goal progress and completion. Integrating technology tools to accomplish this can improve the ease at which school improvement progress can be measured and improve the timeliness and accuracy of response to progress checks. Utilizing technology in other areas such as to facilitate collaboration, administer assessments, and communicate with stakeholders are valuable; however, utilizing technology to collect, organize, and analyze data for school improvement and progress monitoring is most closely related to the implementation of the school improvement plan.

40. C: To partner productively with community members for the shared goal of improving student learning and achievement, schools should take the initiative in offering them information (including school and student data) rather than furnish it only upon request, clearly explain to stakeholders how *all* community members can participate meaningfully, align all collaborative activities directly with the school's vision and goals, and share pertinent, accurate, clear achievement data transparently rather than limiting what they disclose.

41. A: According to research findings, transformational school leaders model and promote staff development and self-improvement by building school structures that encourage staff members to participate in decision-making, delegating responsibilities judiciously as needed, and supporting staff when they operate autonomously. Transformational school leaders encourage teacher autonomy in decision-making, strive to attain full staff consensus rather than overriding staff in determining school priorities, and communicate these priorities to staff and students to develop a strong sense of purpose overall.

42. B: Alternative high school principals (Mohr and Dichter, 2001) identified staff developmental stages of honeymoon, conflict, confusion, messy, scary, and mature, in that order, in becoming learning communities. The honeymoon stage is identified as when a sense of community first emerges. The conflict stage is summarized as "the honeymoon is over." The confusion stage is characterized by staff uncertainty over the leader's role. The messy stage involves increased lack of clarity. The scary stage finds staff wondering where accountability and authority are. The mature stage equates to the birth of a learning community.

43. D: The ultimate responsibility of developing and implementing professional development for teachers and staff belongs to the school leader. However, a school leader should leverage the knowledge and expertise of the administrative team and teacher leaders in this process. The school leader may provide the overall vision and goals and delegate some of the responsibilities relating to professional development to others while holding all parties accountable for meeting goals and aligning to the vision.

44. A: Researchers have found that students' academic self-concepts are *not correlated* with their academic achievement, but *are* correlated with later life successes like employment and earnings. Although socioeconomic status (SES) is related to academic self-concept (as well as achievement and retention), it does *not* correlate as strongly with SES as with students' home educational settings. Although smaller school size is found to benefit student participation as well as principal leadership and teacher distributed leadership, *larger* school size correlates positively with student academic self-concept.

45. D: In a cycle of continuous school improvement driven by data that they collect and analyze, schools and leaders should first conduct a needs assessment for their school to identify where to focus improvement efforts. Once they have identified needs, they should set specific improvement goals. Then they should reflect on their teaching and leading practices for further informing improvement. This enables implementing improvement strategies. Another necessary step is to assess progress during and following implementation.

46. C: Analyzing videos of one's instructional practices is used in self-assessment and can also support reflection. Rather than relying on the observation feedback of a third party, the teacher can self-assess their proficiency in instructional delivery. Writing in a journal is used in reflection, not for self-assessment.

47. B: Although professional development (PD) must be job-embedded and school-based, it can occur even outside of the school building if teachers view it as part of their daily work duties and it emerges from and contributes to daily classroom practice. Teachers must be actively involved in the learning process for effective PD. PD should be student-centered, not teacher-centered because what teachers learn is to support student learning, not for teachers' own sake. Collaborative teacher problem-solving is both valuable and a PD guideline and addresses the issue of teacher isolation and as well as fosters professional and community respect.

48. C: Adults learn in more productive ways when they know they have the right of choice whether to voluntarily learn or not, when they have choices among learning materials, when they are involved in planning the instruction they will be accessing, and when they are able to give instructors input about how their learning will be assessed.

49. A: A school must Manifestation Determination Review within 10 school days according to the following criteria: if the school is seeking to change student placement for more than 10 consecutive days for disciplinary reasons; if the school suspends a student for disciplinary reasons for more than 10 *cumulative,* not consecutive days, *and* for every subsequent suspension, not on a one-time basis; the school is *considering* expelling or otherwise excluding a student for disciplinary reasons rather than already having done so; or the *parent(s)*, not the school, request(s) this meeting after a disciplinary incident.

50. C: Allowing for individual variations, many public-school districts receive the largest proportion of funding from their state government. According to the American Association of School Administrators (AASA), the federal government provides less than 20 percent of the amount that the state government does, with city or other local and intermediate governments combined contributing only slightly less than the state government. Only a very small proportion of funding comes from other sources.

51. C: Cooperative learning, the process of facilitating student collaboration develops social skills, teamwork, individual and collective responsibility, and group interdependence. The Socratic method is useful for facilitating student engagement, assessing student learning, and fostering critical thinking but is not useful for delivering instruction. Project-based learning is useful for active, hands-on learning experiences and does not require technology to be implemented effectively. Technology is a useful tool for delivering instruction, but is not required; technology is also effective when students utilize technology to engage in the learning process, making technology more student-centered.

52. A: Budget planning and operations coordination are two aspects of using technology to support effective school organization management. Notifying stakeholders of meetings is an aspect of using technology to facilitate effective and timely communication. Collecting, disaggregating, and analyzing different school data is an aspect of using technology to manage information. Facilitating multiple stakeholder contributions to projects is an aspect of using technology to enhance collaboration.

53. B: Multiple research studies find that the most effective school leaders are better at identifying the teachers best and worst at increasing student performance among their existing faculty. However, researchers cannot determine whether the fact that effective school leaders also hire the best experienced teachers is more attributable to better leader ability in choosing teachers or to excellent teachers' attraction to schools with the best existing faculty quality. Researchers do observe that school leaders cannot differentiate quality among average teachers as well as they can differentiate better from poorer teachers due to lesser contrast.

54. B: A school leader can best control the quality of the teaching faculty by developing strategies that address strategic hiring, development, and retention of effective teachers. Hiring effective teachers is important therefore due diligence must be made to screen candidates and ensure that they have the appropriate skills needed for the classroom and are compatible with school culture. The school leader must provide the appropriate training and development for teachers so that all can grow professionally. Lastly, the school leader must be intentional about retaining effective teachers to reduce the need for hiring.

55. C: A transactional leader is defined as a leader who is most concerned about performing under the existing policies, rules, and laws. These leaders emphasize compliance and progress toward current goals, often emphasizing strong organizational rigidity and using punishment and reward-based systems of motivation. Transactional leaders are typically able to keep motivation in short term endeavors, but struggle to be adaptable for systemic change. This type of leader is defined in contrast to transformational leaders, who tend to look for possible changes that can be made to improve an existing system. Too much of either leadership style can lead to negative results, so it is recommended to pursue a balance between improving existing systems and striving to perform well within existing systems.

56. A: According to the US Department of Education's Privacy Technical Assistance Center (PTAC) and the National Institute of Standards and Technology (NIST), a school data breach response *policy* defines staff roles and responsibilities; metrics and standards; and reporting, remediation, and feedback mechanisms. Identifying necessary management support and school resources is a function of the data breach response *plan*. Standardizing response tasks and behaviors and preventing errors from being introduced are functions of *procedures* developed based on the plan. Regular risk assessments are a function not of these components but a recommended broader information management strategy.

57. D: The American Psychological Association (APA) recommends a tiered model of behavior management above all others for schools—i.e., a system of positive behavior supports that includes both prevention and intervention with primary, secondary, and tertiary levels—not only for school-wide systems or only for disruptive behaviors of individual students, but for both of these as well as for classroom behavior management.

58. C: An integrated management system unites all digital management systems into one total structure, facilitating shared objectives and working as a unit to achieve them. According to experts, a school not using any digital management system is not the best candidate without experience or systems to integrate. A school using one system and not planning more does not need integration. The ideal school uses one or more systems and plans adding more. Systems within an integrated management system share policies, documentation, processes, and procedures; a school wanting these separated does not want integration.

59. D: New policies should be well communicated in vision and in methodology, but if the policy comes directly from the leadership without having shared motivation the community as a whole will not have buy in and the implementation is likely to face resistance. Delegating authority to staff is a great way of involving stakeholders within the school building but does not include members of the school community who are not employed at the school. Communicating frequently is effective for sharing the vision but does not necessarily motivate community members to participate in implementing new ideas, policies, and procedures.

60. B: In most public-school districts, typically the District Office of Achievement and Accountability makes preliminary enrollment projections to inform school budgets, but not alone because of the difficulty of projecting. Instead, they submit their projections to school leaders, who revise them as needed. School leaders do not project their schools' enrollment alone. Final enrollment projections are made by district committees representing not only the Finance and Student Support offices, but also district Achievement and Accountability and Operations offices.

61. D: The term decentralization refers to the transfer of power and authority from the school districts to principals to make decisions related to budgets and staffing. In centralized school districts, the central office determines campus spending and the principal has little to no control over how funds are used. In decentralized school districts, principals have greater control over how to use the funds allotted to their school campus.

62. C: It is not the school leader's responsibility to interpret federal and state law for application at the school level because this is the responsibility of the school district as articulated in local policy; however, the school leader is responsible for knowing federal and state law. School policies and local laws are developed in accordance with federal and state laws; however, if there is a discrepancy between local policies and federal or state law, the school leader must adhere to federal and state law. Policies are interpretation of law and must be revised and updated regularly to align with state and federal laws. School leaders are their own agents in regard to voting in elections relating to policy.

63. A: According to the National Education Association (NEA), a school acceptable use policy (AUP) should include a preamble explaining need for an AUP; its goals and development; a school conduct code inclusion of online activity; a definition section of important terms; a policy statement of computer services covered and conditions required for student use (e.g., taking a computer responsibility class); an acceptable uses section *and* unacceptable uses section; and a violations and sanctions section, which should tell students how to report policy violations or question policy application (which may conform to the school disciplinary code), not just define violations.

64. B: As of 2013, New Jersey and Wyoming required *all* persons to report child abuse and neglect; all other US states identified specific professionals as mandated reporters. These professions include healthcare and mental health professionals *and* childcare providers; teachers, principals, and other school personnel; social workers, *including* school social workers; law enforcement officers; and medical examiners or coroners.

65. B: School leaders are responsible for ensuring that school safety policies comply with federal, state, and local safety regulations for school physical plants and for communicating all school safety policies to employees, students, and families. They are also responsible for notifying staff and parents in advance of physical plant projects and any other changes that could affect student and staff safety and health. Their responsibilities include developing and revising safety policies with a school health and safety team and other school staff, students, and families, as well as warning parents of painting, pesticides, and other environmental hazards.

66. A: The logistics function of the ICS identifies services and resources for supporting incident response needs. The planning function collects and evaluates information, identifies incident response issues, develops action plans, and recommends future actions. The command function manages incidents overall and is directly responsible for public safety, information, and community response agency liaisons. The operations function develops objectives, organizes resources, and directs actions and resources for incident responses.

67. D: According to the National Center for Education Statistics (NCES), school leaders should *not* ignore the political environment because political support and connections can greatly benefit obtaining funding and legislation. They should avoid overly technical language with most stakeholder audiences who will not understand it industry jargon. Leaders should communicate with stakeholders in sensitive situations. However, leaders should avoid engaging in large-scale open forums which can obstruct progress by being unfocused, unstructured, and may admit too many voices.

68. A: School leaders should not ask students to serve as translators for their parents who do not speak English. Students may be unreliable translators and also should not carry the responsibility of translating, especially in matters that the student may not need to be involved in. For parents who have missed school parent workshops, school leaders can record video of workshops for parents to watch later. They can create inclusive, welcoming, affirming climates by validating, honoring, and thanking family and community members for supporting the school as well as encouraging and maintaining their meaningful involvement. They can assign parent liaisons, which enable parents to access resources and services that the school offers to families.

69. D: To mobilize and develop community school support, school leaders should consider that businesses and community-based organizations use different language than educators, and should learn and speak their languages accordingly. School leaders must not only exchange their visions, missions, wants, and needs with those of prospective community partners and identify where these match, they must moreover identify where they overlap, i.e., shared commonalities despite differences. School leaders must show prospective partners how collaboration benefits them. Potential partners have motivations as varied as the community organizations interested in collaborating with schools.

70. B: Empirical research into effective practices improving schools and student achievement finds that school leaders overcame resistance to change through proactive strategies, including owning and demonstrating continuing commitment, establishing supportive administrative networks, establishing priorities for change, and communicating with others more intentionally.

71. B: All of the data mentioned would be useful for the school leader to analyze; however, data related to student performance, student attendance data, and student promotion rates are the most comprehensive and informative for the development or revision of the school vision and goals. This data can assist in developing goals that are aligned with federal and state accountability requirements. Analyzing data related to teaching staff and the community are important for understanding and improving campus culture and supporting the instructional goals, but are not the most beneficial when compared to student data. Similarly, school accountability ratings can be helpful to analyze but do not provide sufficient information related to current practice and to the areas of deficit that need to be addressed in the school goals.

72. A: The next step after developing the school vision and goals is to develop a plan for implementing them. The plan should be developed prior to presenting the vision and goals to staff and other stakeholders so that, when they are presented, these stakeholders can be informed of their roles and responsibilities related to implementation of the vision and goals. It is important for a school leader to delegate tasks to other leaders on campus in relation to the vision and goals, but the plan must be developed first in order for the leader to know which tasks to delegate.

73. B: In order to obtain diverse perspectives from the internal and external community, the school leader should include as many types of stakeholders as possible in the process. Students and staff make up the internal community. Parents and other community members make up the external community. It is effective practice to engage stakeholders in a variety of ways; however, in this scenario, a survey distributed to students, parents, staff, and community members would solicit the most diversity of perspectives.

74. C: When monitoring goal progress, it is important to examine data, not just identify whether tasks were completed. School leaders should establish regular intervals for reviewing the data related to the goals that have been set. For example, academic performance data may be reviewed according to grading periods whereas attendance data may be reviewed monthly. Electronic data management systems can be helpful; however, automatic notifications for not meeting thresholds may not be received in a timely manner nor indicate whether goal progress is being met or exceeded unless the school leader intentionally reviews the data at regular intervals.

75. A: The first step that a principal should take is to collect information about the resources and strategies currently in place. This well help the principal identify what aspects of the instructional program to keep, adjust, or eliminate. Budgeting and other instructional decisions should not be made until it is determined what the cause of the deficiencies in math are. Additional testing is not necessary because the principal has sufficient data to determine that there is a deficit in math.

76. C: Student growth is the best data point to inform the principal as to whether the math intervention program was effective and should continue to be funded. Student growth can be calculated by comparing student performance in math at the beginning of the school year to their performance at the end of the school year. Although standardized test performance is an important data point, using this data alone will not indicate the efficacy of the program, especially for students who may have grown significantly, but not enough to meet standardized test performance requirements.

77. B: The principal should consider the campus vision and goals when determining how to allocate resources, including technology resources. The first step that a principal should take when considering spending school funds is determining how the purchase will support the achievement of the vision and goals. When considering upgrading or replacing technology, it is appropriate for the principal to evaluate the current condition of the technology or seek ways to save money; however, the first step that should be taken is to determine if the spending is in alignment with the school goals and vision.

78. D: Professional development sessions that take place over time, in contrast to single-session trainings are more likely to have an impact on teacher performance. Additionally, when a cohort of teachers participates in a training, there is opportunity for collaboration and collective accountability. There are benefits of providing individualized professional development opportunities for teachers; however, when these self-paced trainings are not time bound or accompanied by accountability measures, they are less likely to have a direct impact on current teacher performance.

79. A: A school leader must create structures in the school programming that promote collaboration for teachers. Allotting time in the master schedule for co-planning ensures that teachers will have dedicated time to collaborate, such as by participating in professional learning communities. Offering to pay teachers to stay after school may not be effective because some teachers may opt-out. Additionally, these planning sessions could interfere with other school activities these teachers may be involved in, such as coaching or tutoring. Providing asynchronous collaboration online could potentially be helpful, but it is not the best choice since it likely will not lead to real-time collaboration. Removing qualified teachers for planning can negatively impact student performance and should be used sparingly, if at all.

80. C: Providing ongoing feedback to teachers has the most significant impact on teacher performance. School leaders are responsible for evaluating teachers, providing feedback on evaluations, and assisting teachers with improving areas of weakness through coaching, mentoring, professional development and other strategies.

81. D: School leaders must maintain rigorous standards-based instruction across the campus. If students are not able to meet the standards, additional supports and interventions must be offered to students to address educational gaps. The math teacher cannot choose to lower the expectations or standards for students without permission and documentation according to local and state policies. The teacher does not demonstrate a need for training related to implementation of the curriculum, but the teacher must be directed to abide by the curriculum as written.

82. C: Collaboration requires that the school leader engage directly with teachers to maintain an instructional program that delivers standards-based instruction. PLCs are excellent opportunities to listen and provide input during the planning stage for delivering instruction. Auditing classroom materials and analyzing the accuracy of grading are good tools for evaluating the delivery of standards-based instruction but are not collaborative. Administering a survey about new curriculum is not collaborative and does not help to support implementation of current materials.

83. A: The school leader should make time to collect and analyze student work samples. The audit can be random or the school leader can focus on particular groups of students based on data; however, the school leader should discuss the work samples with the teachers who assigned them. Monitoring grades does not provide the school leader with information about the assignments that were graded. Hosting a science fair and using portfolios for assessment can be beneficial but do not directly indicate that the school leader is involved in these activities.

84. B: The dean should ask teachers what resources they would like and purchase as many of their suggestions as possible for all teachers. This would increase the number of resources available to teachers and offer them a variety of resources to choose from. Requiring teachers to purchase materials on their own is a disincentive if teachers cannot afford the upfront cost. Professional development is not a resource, it is training. Seeking free or discounted materials does not guarantee that the number and variety of resources will increase on campus if there are limited to no resources available in the local area.

85. D: Students must have rigorous instruction in the classroom to be prepared for challenging curriculum in the future. Students who perform well in class but perform poorly on standardized assessments are evidence of misalignment of course work to standardized assessments or inadequate levels of rigor in the classroom. Evaluating the grades of one grade level of students in a specific class is not evidence of ensuring all students are prepared for a challenging curriculum. Reviewing one assessment that was administered prior to enrollment in the school does not demonstrate ongoing monitoring.

86. B: Reading and writing skills are best taught and reinforced within the context of subject matter content. Creating a cross-curricular focus on reading and writing skills would best address the gap in performance among students who are not reading on grade level. Increasing opportunities for students to read is beneficial, but is less effective in closing opportunity gaps, especially when opportunities to engage in reading are voluntary such as after school or at home. Targeted test preparation has limited efficacy if attendance is voluntary and student performance is not monitored.

87. C: The best action that the principal can take to increase the frequency of classroom observations is to plan the observations into the schedule each week. This will force all other appointments and meetings to be scheduled around the classroom observations. Classroom visits should not be left to chance or they will likely not be conducted due to the many tasks that a principal may have to address throughout the day. Additionally, the principal should aim to visit classrooms on different days of the week and times of the day to obtain a well-rounded perspective of teaching and learning on campus.

88. A: The best strategy the principal can use to establish a continuous improvement cycle is to assess students at regular intervals and adjust instruction based on the data. Benchmark exams are typically shorter assessments over selected objectives rather than large comprehensive assessments. Data from these assessments reflect the mastery of objectives that are recently taught and are aligned to the pacing of the curriculum scope and sequence. Testing in less frequent intervals can also be helpful if the data is used to adjust instruction immediately rather than informing plans for the subsequent school year.

89. C: It is critical for the school leader to communicate progress toward the school vision and goals to the school community and other stakeholders within the community. The vision and goals outline the direction and focus of the school and all other activities must align to the vision and goals. Activities such as volunteering, mentoring, and collaborating should be in alignment with the school vision and goals; therefore, it is most important for stakeholders to be informed of the school vision and goals and how the school is making progress in these areas.

90. D: The school leader must personally verify the condition of the plant facility to ensure that the facility is in good condition and compliant with safety regulations. Communicating with the plant operator regularly, requesting that staff inform the leader of physical working conditions, and maintaining official documents are important, but do not substitute for the leader's responsibility to verify what is reported or documented.

91. A: Each of the suggestions are viable options for the school leader to implement; however, the school leader needs to know why teachers leave or plan to leave in order to best address the problem. Seeking feedback from the teaching staff can help the school leader to focus resources on the most direct causes of teacher attrition. Once the causes are identified, the school leader can determine if the other suggestions are applicable.

92. C: Creating a grief counseling group in response to the death of a student is a positive action, but is reactive, not proactive. An education leader cannot predict every occurrence that may impact student mental and emotional health, but the education leader can create processes and structures that can support students ongoing emotional safety. These can include designing referral systems for mental health care, providing information about available resources to students and their parents, and using school resources to provide mental health support.

93. B: The action that would best address the challenges in communication, parental engagement, and at home learning is to help the parents learn English by offering ESL classes on campus. Hosting the classes on campus encourages parents to engage with the school community and reinforces that the school values the presence and engagement of the parents. Having a translator on campus and translating documents for parents are important actions to take but are not long-term solutions to the challenge. Students should not be asked to translate school information for their parents.

94. A: It is the responsibility of the school principal to establish processes and procedures that protect students and the confidentiality of their information and monitors the use of those procedures. This breach of student confidentiality could have posed a safety risk of the student; the attendance clerk violated policy and law by providing the student's information over the telephone without verify who they were speaking to. Even though the attendance clerk failed to adhere to policy, it is ultimately the principal's responsibility to ensure that all staff are trained on policies affecting student rights and confidentiality and adhere to those policies.

95. D: An effective school leader is transparent when making decisions. This transparency includes sharing data and/or rationale for making decisions. The school leader has already determined that the fine arts program should be discontinued so the best action for the principal to take next is to explain the rationale for that decision to the school community.

96. C: Excluding a student from engaging in a campus-based activity based on gender is unethical and prohibited. First the principal should speak to the teacher about their bias as this bias may affect other aspects of the teacher's role beyond the after-school club. Afterwards, the principal can require that the sponsor allow the male student to participate; however, the principal must first address the beliefs held by the teacher.

97. B: Recognizing and celebrating educational success is an effective strategy to develop positive family and community partnerships. A school leader should make an effort to organize events on campus and in the community to develop positive partnerships. Live events facilitate two-way communication, unlike newsletters which are one-way modes of communication. Attending athletic events and soliciting feedback from the community are additional ways to build a relationship with the community, but the most effective strategy for building a positive partnership is to host an event that spotlights positive things related to the school and students.

98. C: It is beneficial to students and the community to build mutually beneficial relationships with various organizations in the community, including medical clinics. The school leader is responsible for ensuring there is documentation of these relationships, such as a memorandum of understanding, logs, or other forms of recordkeeping to document the nature of these relationships and to whom services are provided. The school leader should ensure that there is equitable access to these resources as determined by law, school policy, and the nature of the services provided.

99. D: While school leaders promote a college-bound culture, they also know that students should be prepared for the career of their choice, which may require specialized training or preparation other than traditional college. In this scenario, the school leader should analyze employment data for the community that the school serves and determine if trends in the data justify adding or changing school programming to meet the needs of the community.

100. A: Cultural diversity can affect academic achievement of students for a variety of reasons, including language barriers, cultural bias in curriculum, cultural bias in instructional practices and much more. If a particular demographic of students is not succeeding, the school leader must identify what the barriers to achievement are by talking with teachers, students, parents, and even community members. The school leader must then address those barriers by engaging diverse team members to meet the needs of all students on campus.

Constructed Response

1. Essay question graders commonly look for the following elements in a strong response: strong content knowledge, clear organization, and effective arguments or examples. Language and usage are not usually strictly graded, but can make a big impact on the clarity of your ideas.

Please use the provided rubric to make sure your response meets these common criteria. Try to have a friend or family member grade your response for you or take a break after writing your response and return to grade it with fresh eyes.

Constructed Response Rubric

Domain	Description
Content Knowledge	• The response directly addresses every part of the prompt. • The response demonstrates independent knowledge of the topic. • The response discusses the topic at an appropriate depth.
Organization	• The response introduces the topic, usually with a thesis statement or by restating the prompt. • The response directly addresses the prompt by providing a clear and concise answer or solution. • The answer or solution is supported by logical arguments or evidence. • The response restates the main idea in the conclusion.
Arguments and Examples	• The response provides a reasonable answer to the prompt. • The answer is supported by strong reasoning or evidence. • The response develops ideas logically and connects ideas to one another. • The reasoning and evidence provided act to support a unified main idea.
Language and Usage	• The response demonstrates effective use of grammar and uses varied sentence structure throughout the response. • The response demonstrates correct use of spelling, punctuation, and capitalization. • The response demonstrates strong and varied use of vocabulary relevant to the topic and appropriate for the intended audience.

2. Essay question graders commonly look for the following elements in a strong response: strong content knowledge, clear organization, and effective arguments or examples. Language and usage are not usually strictly graded, but can make a big impact on the clarity of your ideas.

Please use the provided rubric to make sure your response meets these common criteria. Try to have a friend or family member grade your response for you or take a break after writing your response and return to grade it with fresh eyes.

Constructed Response Rubric

Domain	Description
Content Knowledge	• The response directly addresses every part of the prompt. • The response demonstrates independent knowledge of the topic. • The response discusses the topic at an appropriate depth.
Organization	• The response introduces the topic, usually with a thesis statement or by restating the prompt. • The response directly addresses the prompt by providing a clear and concise answer or solution. • The answer or solution is supported by logical arguments or evidence. • The response restates the main idea in the conclusion.
Arguments and Examples	• The response provides a reasonable answer to the prompt. • The answer is supported by strong reasoning or evidence. • The response develops ideas logically and connects ideas to one another. • The reasoning and evidence provided act to support a unified main idea.
Language and Usage	• The response demonstrates effective use of grammar and uses varied sentence structure throughout the response. • The response demonstrates correct use of spelling, punctuation, and capitalization. • The response demonstrates strong and varied use of vocabulary relevant to the topic and appropriate for the intended audience.

3. Essay question graders commonly look for the following elements in a strong response: strong content knowledge, clear organization, and effective arguments or examples. Language and usage are not usually strictly graded, but can make a big impact on the clarity of your ideas.

Please use the provided rubric to make sure your response meets these common criteria. Try to have a friend or family member grade your response for you or take a break after writing your response and return to grade it with fresh eyes.

Constructed Response Rubric

Domain	Description
Content Knowledge	• The response directly addresses every part of the prompt. • The response demonstrates independent knowledge of the topic. • The response discusses the topic at an appropriate depth.
Organization	• The response introduces the topic, usually with a thesis statement or by restating the prompt. • The response directly addresses the prompt by providing a clear and concise answer or solution. • The answer or solution is supported by logical arguments or evidence. • The response restates the main idea in the conclusion.
Arguments and Examples	• The response provides a reasonable answer to the prompt. • The answer is supported by strong reasoning or evidence. • The response develops ideas logically and connects ideas to one another. • The reasoning and evidence provided act to support a unified main idea.
Language and Usage	• The response demonstrates effective use of grammar and uses varied sentence structure throughout the response. • The response demonstrates correct use of spelling, punctuation, and capitalization. • The response demonstrates strong and varied use of vocabulary relevant to the topic and appropriate for the intended audience.

Practice Test #2

Multiple Choice Questions

1. When utilizing school data to inform school vision, mission, and goals, which of the following data should school leaders analyze?

a. Historical data from standardized tests
b. Data from formative assessments
c. Course grades, promotion, and retention rates
d. Data from formative and summative assessments and community survey results

2. In many public-school districts, students with certain linguistic and/or cultural backgrounds are disproportionately enrolled in special education programs. How can a school leader best address this type of overrepresentation?

a. Examine current school procedures for assigning grade levels to students
b. Examine instructional strategies targeting students referred to special education
c. Examine instruments used to evaluate student need for special education
d. Examine the curriculum and related expectations of student achievement

3. A staff member who used to perform their job consistently begins completing tasks after due dates and has started being absent without a reasonable excuse. Which of the following describes a school leader's best course of action to address this staff member?

a. The school leader should give some of the staff member's responsibilities to someone else who is more reliable.
b. The school leader should recommend that the staff member seek mental health and counseling services.
c. The staff member should be terminated.
d. The staff member should be transferred to another department.

4. According to research related to the factors that contribute to the success of higher-performing public schools, which of the following is true?

a. The school leader is the single defining success factor
b. School success is based on a complex set of interrelated factors
c. Schools cannot be successful without additional funding
d. Factors related to curriculum and instruction are the most important determinants of success

5. Which of the following best describes the relationship between the school principal and the school board?

a. The school principal recommends the hiring and termination of teachers to the school board.
b. The school principal reports campus data to the school board at board meetings.
c. The school board elects or hires and supervises the superintendent, who in turns hires and supervises the school principal.
d. The school board implements state and local policies that the principal must abide by.

6. Which of the following is an appropriate example of an action that school leaders can take to change negative school cultures and employee attitudes that interfere with realizing school visions?

a. Observe indicators of school culture among students and staff
b. Design professional development sessions for teachers that address school culture
c. Frequently recount successful accomplishments of goals related to school vision
d. Hold annual ceremonies for celebrating successes

7. On which of the following should educators mainly base their education practices?

a. Traditions in educational practice
b. Educators' personal experiences
c. Action research
d. Peer-reviewed research and best practices

8. A school is in the process of implementing a campus-wide adoption of new technology. Which of the following is LEAST central to the role of a school leader acting to implement this change?

a. Leading by example and using technology with teachers and students.
b. Attending professional development classes and keeping current with the research.
c. Establishing conditions for change by setting high learning expectations and encouraging teacher effort.
d. Encouraging use of the new technology, offering teachers learning opportunities, and resolving implementation problems.

9. Which of the following accurately reflects evaluative criteria that school leaders should consider first when deciding to utilize community resources to support student learning?

a. Congruence with the school's vision and mission.
b. Immediate impact on student achievement.
c. Results from prior implementation.
d. The relationship of the person or organization to the school.

10. Which of the following is the best example of how school leaders can support teachers in developing their expertise and leadership skills?

a. School leaders should increase teachers' workloads to give them opportunity to demonstrate responsibility.
b. School leaders should develop all teachers in the same way to avoid building resentment among staff.
c. School leaders must create safe environments for teachers' risk-taking and creative ideas.
d. School leaders should limit how much authority to share with teachers to prevent diminishing their own authority.

11. According to some school consensus-building models, which of these is most typical?

a. One hundred percent of faculty must agree to implement what is proposed 100 percent of the time.
b. Dissenting members can opt out of the implementation.
c. If consensus seems impossible, having 80 percent of members agree is not enough.
d. Those dissenting must agree not to obstruct and to support implementation.

12. School leaders must know of a wide range of mental health professionals available to students. To which of the following are students most often referred for help that schools cannot provide?

a. Career counselors
b. Family counselors
c. Group counselors
d. School counselors

13. Among the following personnel who may work in a public school, which of the following would likely be campus-based personnel?

a. A bus driver
b. A counselor
c. A food service worker
d. A school psychologist

14. Which of the following is true about mental health and student learning and achievement?

a. Educational problems are not related to mental health issues.
b. External stressors can create obstacles to learning and achievement.
c. Only psychological disorders diagnosed by a health professional can be addressed in schools.
d. Only students who qualify for special education services can receive support for mental health issues.

15. Which of the following does not pertain to the development of a shared school vision?

a. Ensuring that the vision is applicable to the whole community
b. Hosting community meetings to communicate the school vision
c. Surveying community members to receive insight
d. Collecting data to support an ideal outcome

16. What is the most accurate definition of a learning objective?

a. What educators hope to accomplish during their instruction
b. What educators are supposed instruct the students
c. What students expect teachers to instruct them
d. What educators expect students to be able to do via instruction

17. Of the following, which is true about multiple assessments of student learning?

a. Different assessment types access different skills and learning styles.
b. Students must be re-tested often or they forget what they learned.
c. Summative assessments following instruction are typically sufficient.
d. Summative assessments enable adjusting instruction as it continues.

18. Which of the following best describes what school leaders should consider when identifying professional development for staff?

a. Individual staff members' goals are most important.
b. School goals and vision always take precedence.
c. Individual staff member and school goals are of equal importance.
d. Professional development is primarily for accountability purposes and goals.

19. Which of the following is true about school leaders as role models for teachers in professional development (PD)?

a. School leaders should facilitate PD activities.
b. School leaders should participate in PD with teachers.
c. School leaders should monitor teacher implementation of learning from PD sessions.
d. School leaders should determine the PD offered to teachers.

20. An elementary school leader has set a goal of establishing a school climate wherein all educators believe every child can learn and succeed, and are committed to enabling every child to do so. Which classroom practice should the leader encourage teachers to use toward this goal?

a. Differentiating instruction
b. Assigning student teams to compete in contests
c. Differentiating assessment standards by student
d. Regularly researching individual student interests

21. Advanced technology integration in schools includes empowering students to engage in the learning process using technology. Which of the following best exemplifies students creating content using digital media?

a. Students access wiki pages to review lesson materials
b. Students record themselves reading aloud for reading assessment
c. Students design elaborate digital storybooks to prepare for a state writing exam
d. Students create PowerPoint presentations about insects using photos from the internet

22. Which statement is accurate about why classroom management systems are effective?

a. By making learning environments orderly, they enable student academic success.
b. They control student behavior rather than helping emotional-social development.
c. They work by increasing prosocial behavior rather than academic engagement.
d. They work by providing individualized intensive interventions for all students.

23. Surveyed school principals have reported that which of the following has been adversely affected since standards-based accountability systems were implemented?

a. Teacher morale
b. Curriculum and instruction
c. Student assessment practices
d. Expectations and achievement

24. Which of the following is true regarding how teacher evaluation standards should be designed?

a. Teacher evaluations should reference clear instructional standards to prioritize student learning.
b. Teacher evaluations should be conducted by school leaders with a single standardized measure.
c. Teacher evaluations should be based on occasional observation and avoid critical commentaries.
d. Teacher evaluations should play a minor part in important decisions about teacher employment.

25. Which of the following is true regarding information and data that teachers should consider when planning for differentiated instruction?

a. Special population identification and past academic performance are the only data that teachers should consider when planning for differentiated instruction.
b. Formative assessment is not useful when planning for differentiated instruction.
c. Student interests should be a major determining factor when planning for differentiated instruction.
d. Student performance data, interests, and learning styles should all be considered when planning for differentiated instruction.

26. Which kind of data best helps teachers to identify strengths and needs in their teaching practices, support capacity-building, and identify specific remedial student groups?

a. Formative data
b. Summative data
c. Student profiles
d. Enrollment data

27. To inform professional development methods, which of the following is the best format for adult learners, based on the principles of adult learning?

a. Formal
b. Directive
c. Hands-on
d. Theoretical

28. Which of the following is true about the efficacy of new teacher induction programs on schools?

a. They make new teachers more comfortable, not more effective.
b. They increase the rates at which the new teachers are retained.
c. They enhance teacher instructional skills, not teacher leadership.
d. They help education inequities more than student achievement.

29. Which of the following should NOT be considered when a school principal observes teachers in their classrooms?

a. The quality and rigor of assignments given to students.
b. The implementation of strategies learned in professional development sessions.
c. Classroom environment and culture.
d. The teacher's tenure or contract status.

30. Which of the following best describes how the school leader should evaluate the technology data systems they use?

a. Does the data system provide the data necessary to support the work of collaborative data teams?
b. Is the technology data system affordable?
c. Is the technology data system user friendly?
d. Do other schools use this technology data system?

31. Which of the following is most accurate about effective and appropriate school and co-curricular activities to prepare high school students for college and careers?

a. Career and technical education can only be obtained in magnet or technical schools.
b. School partnerships with higher education institutions best prepare students for jobs.
c. Community-based and project-based learning prepare students for higher education.
d. High school curricula should be pertinent to student lives, communities, and cultures.

32. The federal Supportive School Discipline Initiative (SSDI) issued a (2014) positive school discipline guidance package. Why did the US Department of Justice (DOJ) collaborate with the US Department of Education (ED) in producing this resource?

a. To make school discipline consistent with justice and correctional systems.
b. To address inevitable student justice involvement by disciplinary exclusion.
c. To ensure that Civil Rights Act titles prohibiting discrimination are enforced.
d. To establish disciplinary practices to keep juvenile offenders out of school.

33. Which of the following most accurately reflects how school leaders can identify and decrease educational and institutional bias and discriminatory practices?

a. Establishing anti-discrimination rules and identify a campus leader to enforce them.
b. Establish an anti-discrimination policy and form a committee to find opportunities to learn about and promote other cultures.
c. Hire a culturally diverse leadership team and have them speak to staff and students about their cultures.
d. Include opportunities in the curriculum for students to learn about other cultures.

34. Which of the following would be the most effective way to engage parents in student behavior management systems?

a. Distribute the behavioral code of conduct to parents at the beginning of the school year.
b. Find parent volunteers to help enforce the behavioral code of conduct.
c. Ask for feedback from parents on the draft of the behavioral code of conduct before it is finalized.
d. Develop a behavioral code of conduct in partnership with teachers, parents, and students.

35. What does research into school mental health show about collaboration with the community?

a. Clinical psychiatric care and other services are not practicable or suitable in schools.
b. A cohesive continuum of intervention must primarily address severe mental health problems.
c. School staff must work with families and service providers rather than policymakers.
d. An integrated intervention continuum must mainly address universal student need.

36. A school leader is managing a significant structural change on campus. Which of the following strategies would be most effective in managing change?

a. Develop goals related to the new changes.
b. Obtain buy in from stakeholders by allowing them to have input.
c. Provide professional development opportunities that will equip teachers to be successful with the new changes.
d. Replace staff who are not on board with the changes.

37. In school-wide positive behavior support programs, which level typically involves school-wide practices that support positive behaviors for all students?

a. Tier 1
b. Tier 2
c. Tier 3
d. Tier 4

38. What is most accurate regarding social and emotional learning (SEL) programs that schools often offer in conjunction with school-wide positive behavior support (SPBS) programs?

a. Programming is implemented at individual grade levels.
b. Programming requires quarterly monitoring.
c. Programming includes practicing opportunities.
d. Programming is limited to the school environment.

39. Which of the following statements correctly reflects considerations for school leaders in supporting school improvement through effective resource management?

a. The school vision and goals are most dependent upon physical resources.
b. Material resources are priority as they are needed for a safe, comfortable teaching and learning environment.
c. Managing fiscal resources is necessary for managing other resources, with some exceptions.
d. Managing human resources is necessary for smaller class sizes and optimal student learning and achievement.

40. When using student outcome data to monitor school improvement progress, which of these would indicate a need to update the school improvement plan?

a. Data show improvement goals taking longer to be met than planned.
b. Data show that the school is on target to meet expected goals.
c. Data is able to be monitored more frequently due to acquisition of improved technology applications.
d. Data show that the school lags behind other schools with similar student populations.

41. According to research findings, transformational school leaders are most effective in promoting organizational learning. Which of the following best reflects how they do this?

a. By demonstrating their high expectations for students.
b. By demonstrating their high expectations for teachers.
c. By modeling ongoing learning and providing opportunities for staff to learn from peers.
d. By researching effective instructional practices and training staff to implement them.

42. Which of the following accurately describes cognitive and affective processes involved in school organizational learning and staff development?

a. Conversation and affirmation are cognitive, reflection and invitation are affective.
b. Reflection and conversation are cognitive, affirmation and invitation are affective.
c. Reflection and affirmation are cognitive, conversation and invitation are affective.
d. Affirmation and invitation are cognitive, reflection and conversation are affective.

43. Which of the following best describes the relationship between school leadership and student outcomes?

a. School leadership is directly related to student outcomes.
b. School leadership is indirectly related to student outcomes.
c. School leadership is not related to student outcomes.
d. There is not enough research to determine the nature of the relationship.

44. What is most true about effective new teacher induction programs?

a. They should focus on supporting new teachers but not leaders.
b. They should give only new teachers professional development.
c. They should use self-assessments and reflection for teachers to measure performance.
d. They should improve student achievement via teacher efficacy.

45. Of the following, which correctly reflects characteristics of school professional development that will best meet student needs and achieve school goals?

a. It should be provided exclusively to professional teachers and faculty.
b. It should be separated from the job to enable greater perspective.
c. It should be differentiated to address individual areas of challenge.
d. It should be provided periodically but regularly by being scheduled.

46. Research shows that school leaders' time spent on which of these does *not* predict better student achievement?

a. Making evaluations.
b. Class walkthroughs.
c. Coaching teachers.
d. Program development.

47. Which of the following represents a principle informing school leader support and professional development (PD) of teachers throughout their careers?

a. PD must be continuing and supported by repetition and follow-up to change teaching over time.
b. PD for teachers should be focused on practice and not on theoretical bases.
c. PD is best administered as a stand-alone process within individual schools.
d. When school leaders furnish PD, they should be sure to include the newest, most popular topics.

48. Which of the following describes a role of parents and other community members as it relates to educator professional development (PD)?

a. Holding educators accountable for results.
b. Understanding which student learning needs present difficulties for educators.
c. Demanding and supporting quality PD that improves teaching, leadership, and achievement.
d. Allotting time and facilitating PD that will help educators address student learning problems.

49. In a manifestation determination meeting, if a school Individualized Education Program (IEP) committee determines a student's behavior was a manifestation of his or her disability, what correctly identifies an area the IEP committee will address through a suitable plan?

a. Modifying implementation of the IEP other than how it is written.
b. Adding accommodations, services, etc.without changing the IEP.
c. Offering additional services as needed without more evaluations.
d. Making a functional behavior assessment to inform intervention.

50. When school leaders and school district personnel plan school budgets according to budget allocations issued by their school district, which of the following is correct?

a. It is most difficult to project employee salaries for the next school year.
b. Employee benefits are more difficult to predict than employee salaries.
c. Transportation expenses are included in budgets as these are essential.
d. School districts cannot reserve funds for unplanned emergency repairs.

51. According to experts, applying systems thinking to school organizations results in which of these characteristics?

a. Policies and practices of school systems are improved continuously.
b. Curricula become diversified within the school system.
c. School systems become independent of other community systems.
d. Priorities are identified for the success of targeted student groups.

52. A principal has led the school in applying databases, word processing programs, spreadsheet programs, and other application software to solve problems, manage information, and create sophisticated products. This is most related to which purpose of technology use in schools?

a. Using technology as a productivity tool.
b. Using technology as information access.
c. Using technology as a cognitive stimulus.
d. Using technology as instruction content.

53. According to experts, which of the following is the most important factor in how school leaders evaluate their teachers?

a. Being motivated to evaluate teachers.
b. Making time for regular observations.
c. Making time for longer observations.
d. Making evaluations discrete events.

54. Which of the following best describes how school leaders of more effective schools assign students to new (i.e., novice or beginning) teachers, compared to their more experienced colleagues?

a. In more effective schools, new teachers are assigned students with lower achievement.
b. In more effective schools, new teachers are assigned students with higher achievement.
c. In more effective schools, new teachers are assigned randomly relative to achievement.
d. In more effective schools, new teachers are assigned students with similar achievement.

55. Which of the following statements does not support standardized classroom practices and procedures?

a. Improving the cost-efficiency of school programs by reducing differentiation.
b. Increasing the conformity to curricula within departments.
c. Promoting safety throughout the school.
d. Ensuring that students can expect the same teaching style from each teacher.

56. A school's crisis response plan includes a "command and control" framework identifying personnel responsible for directing crisis response. What must school leaders assure most to make this aspect of the plan as effective as possible?

a. Select members from longest-term employees with most school operations' familiarity.
b. During a crisis, distribute leadership of command and control among several members.
c. Clearly define responsibilities for each identified member in advance for various crises.
d. During a crisis, have each command and control member report to at least two others.

57. Which of the following is an accurate statement about tiered behavior management systems used with classrooms and/or individual students?

a. Classroom behavior management systems should start at the beginning of the school year.
b. Individual programs for disruptive student behavior must start at the beginning of the school year.
c. Classroom behavior management systems are applied for a school year, not across grades.
d. Once students know expectations early on, classroom management systems can be faded.

58. What does the National Association of Secondary School Principals (NASSP) recommend regarding effectively using community support outside the school to promote student mental health (MH)?

a. Providing community service personnel in schools' comprehensive staff development is excluded.
b. Providing school staff training in promoting positive school-wide environments is found ineffective.
c. Providing school staff training in how to use mechanisms to refer students to community services is effective.
d. Providing training in early identification of MH disorders and risks excludes community staff in schools.

59. According to the National School Boards Association (NSBA), which of the following reflects an unintended consequence of the Healthy, Hunger-Free Kids Act (2010)?

a. School districts are not committed to giving students healthy nutrition.
b. Many school districts cannot afford the higher costs of new standards.
c. This legislation provides all funding for compliance with its regulations.
d. Students are going hungry because the regulations limit food amounts.

60. A female member of a school's staff sends a letter to the principal. Her complaint is that her supervisor, who is male, calls her and other female employees by names such as "dear", "honey," and so on. The writer of the letter perceives this as disrespectful. In following up, the principal discovers the content of the complaint is confirmed as fact but also that the majority of the rest of the female staff do not perceive the male supervisor as disrespectful in his forms of address. Which action regarding the complaint would be most appropriate?

a. Telling the letter writer that other females on the school staff do not agree with her about the names.
b. Telling the supervisor that some staff are offended, and that referring to female employees in this manner is unprofessional.
c. Calling a meeting of female school staff and their supervisor to review laws on workplace sexual harassment.
d. Calling a meeting with the supervisor to reprimand him asking him to make a public apology to staff.

61. How can school leaders problem-solve and plan for best allocating monetary and material resources to realize school goals for students in economically challenging times?

a. By postponing improvements to the school until some future date.
b. By making cuts in funds allocated to student services and programs.
c. By ending programs identified as not helping student performance.
d. By eliminating professional development opportunities.

62. Which of the following categories represents the highest percentage of budgetary expenditures for public schools?

a. Student support services.
b. Operations.
c. Instruction and instruction related.
d. Administration.

63. Which choice accurately reflects the school leader's role regarding laws protecting student rights to privacy and confidentiality of their educational records?

a. School leaders are responsible for knowing these rights but not enforcing them.
b. School leaders are responsible to enforce these but need not know exceptions.
c. School leaders are responsible for third-party disclosure but not written consent.
d. School leaders are responsible for policy on non-student and parent records access.

64. Regarding acceptable use policies (AUPs) for student Internet access in public schools, which statement is most applicable?

a. The most important factor is the fundamental right of Americans to information access.
b. School district AUPs always require student agreement and parental permission forms.
c. A workable school AUP should achieve a balance between freedom and responsibility.
d. Schools should not consult outside organizations about digital freedom of information.

65. To submit a budget to the school district office, a school leader must specify what resources the school will need to administer toward its instructional program for English language learner (ELL) students in the coming fiscal year. What should the leader's *initial* step be?

a. Identifying the percentage of district funds allocated in the last fiscal year for the ELL program
b. Identifying federal and state program requirements and basing resource calculations on these.
c. Projecting resource amounts required for maintaining other school programs' current funding.
d. Evaluating the effectiveness of the school ELL instructional program for students participating.

66. For managing school food services, the FDA refers to seven Hazard Analysis and Critical Control Point (HACCP) principles. Which of the following lists these principles in the correct sequence?

a. Identifying CCPs, determining critical limits to control hazards, hazard analysis, planning corrective actions, establishing CCP monitoring procedures, record-keeping system, verification procedures.
b. Hazard analysis, identifying CCPs, determining critical limits to control hazards, establishing CCP monitoring procedures, planning corrective actions, verification procedures, record-keeping system.
c. Verification procedures, determining critical limits to control hazards, identifying CCPs, establishing CCP monitoring procedures, hazard analysis, record-keeping system, verification procedures, planning corrective actions.
d. Determining critical limits to control hazards, identifying CCPs, establishing CCP monitoring procedures, verification procedures, record-keeping system, planning corrective actions, hazard analysis.

67. When leaders advocate for their schools in writing, which kind of writing skills do they need to recount true success stories about school initiatives and programs?

a. Persuasive writing skills.
b. Descriptive writing skills.
c. Narrative writing skills.
d. Expository writing skills.

68. School leaders and teachers are frequently frustrated about lack of family and community school involvement, particularly in diverse populations. Which is the most likely source of difficulty?

a. Educator attitudes are often unrealistic.
b. Educators attempt to use too many methods.
c. Educator efforts are often very intense.
d. Educator engagement is lacking.

69. Which of the following informs how school leaders can incorporate diverse family and community aspirations and expectations into their educational decision-making and planning?

a. Family aspirations for children vary markedly by culture.
b. Ethnicity strongly influences family academic aspiration.
c. Income affects family expectations more than race does.
d. Studies find high family aspirations across demographics.

70. What is a result of school leaders' community outreach for partnerships with schools?

a. Community partners are more informed about schools, but do not feel ownership.
b. Community partners who personally help students learn do not expect any thanks because of mutual benefits.
c. Community access to school facilities only benefits the community, not the school.
d. Community members understand schools better by accessing their facilities and events.

71. Which of the following criteria would best help a school leader to determine if the school vision and goals are appropriate?

a. The vision and goals address the areas of deficit determined by analysis of multiple sources of data.
b. The vision and goals are approved by community stakeholders.
c. The vision and goals reflect a balance of the school's strengths and weaknesses.
d. The vision and goals mirror those established by schools with similar performance history and student demographics.

72. A new principal hosts a meeting with community stakeholders to share ideas about the new vision and goals for the school. One of the community members insists that the school focus on improving the school's fine arts program. Which of the following should the new principal consider before including the fine arts program in the vision and goals for the school?

a. How many students are currently participating in the fine arts program?
b. Does the school have the appropriate staff to implement a successful fine arts program?
c. Does focusing on the fine arts program align with district, state, and federal policies and accountability standards?
d. Does the school have the financial resources to support an expanded fine arts program?

73. Which of the following strategies would most likely encourage stakeholders to support and implement the school vision and goals?

a. Announcing the school vision and goals at a community meeting.
b. Publishing the school vision and goals on the school website.
c. Including internal and external community members in the development of the vision and goals.
d. Selecting representatives from the staff and from the community to be advocates for the school's vision and goals.

74. At the midway point of the school year, the school leader is surprised to find that the school is not on track to achieve the school goals for the year. What could the school leader have done to prevent being surprised by this information?

a. Established a plan for assessing and monitoring progress at regular intervals.
b. Delegated responsibilities to the leadership team.
c. Communicated the goals more effectively to stakeholders.
d. Created a committee to engage with the leader in the development of the goals.

75. The sixth-grade math department meets as a professional learning community and determines that overall students in sixth grade are not performing well on the same three math objectives. However, these same students are performing satisfactorily on other math objectives. Which of the following is the most likely reason that the sixth-grade students are not mastering the identified math objectives?

a. The math teachers are ineffective in teaching the identified math objectives.
b. The curriculum is not properly aligned to address the identified math objectives.
c. The students need additional tutoring to master the identified math objectives.
d. The assessment used to measure student performance was biased.

76. An elementary school conducted a pilot of a reading program over the summer and the principal must decide whether to purchase the program for implementation during the regular school year. Which of the following data points would best inform the principal's decision?

a. Feedback from the teachers who implemented the program during the summer.
b. Feedback from the students who participated in the program during the summer.
c. Student scores on assessments included in the reading program.
d. Percentage of growth in reading performance from the beginning of the program until the conclusion of the program.

77. The PTO president expressed concern to the school principal about the recent announcement to purchase new science curriculum for ninth and tenth grade students. He expressed that there was a greater need for college preparation materials for students. Which of the following responses from the principal is best?

a. Purchasing science curriculum was the economic choice because it will benefit a greater number of students for a smaller cost.
b. College preparation materials will be considered for purchase for the upcoming school year.
c. Student performance data demonstrates that students are already performing at a satisfactory level on college entrance exams.
d. One of the school goals for the year is to improve student performance in science and the curriculum purchase supports that goal.

78. Which of the following strategies best addresses the achievement gap?

a. Disaggregating student data by subpopulations to identify disparities in performance.
b. Providing targeted interventions to students who perform unsatisfactorily.
c. Tracking student performance and making projections about future performance based on past performance.
d. Exempting struggling students from meeting certain standards.

79. A new school principal administered a survey to school staff to assess the perceived culture of the school. The data from the survey showed that most of the staff felt that all ideas for the school came from the top and were forced down. The school principal wants to shift the culture and encourage staff to be innovative. Which of the following strategies would best help the principal to meet this goal?

a. Create action committees made up of teachers and staff and give the committees time and resources to generate solutions to campus needs.
b. Place a suggestion box in the teachers' lounge and encourage teachers to submit their ideas for consideration.
c. Inform the staff that there are positions on the Shared Decision-Making Committee for teachers and that they would feel more represented if they engaged in the process.
d. Host a town hall meeting and allow participants to share their ideas publicly.

80. Which of the following strategies is least likely to improve teacher practice?

a. Conducting regular classroom observations and providing written feedback to teachers.
b. Pairing novice teachers with an experienced teacher for peer coaching.
c. Providing teachers with aggregated student performance data each grading cycle.
d. Facilitating professional learning communities for teacher collaboration by grade level and by content area.

81. An assistant principal analyzes student performance data for the grading period and notices that a class of students consistently performs well in Reading and has not demonstrated growth. What might this data suggest?

a. The data is evidence of academic dishonesty.
b. The students may need more rigorous instruction.
c. The teacher is ineffective.
d. Classroom instruction and assessment are unaligned.

82. Which of the following actions best exemplifies a focus on school-wide rigorous curriculum and standards-based instruction?

a. Increase the number of advanced placement and dual credit courses offered on the master schedule.
b. Increase the number of students taking college entrance exams.
c. Evaluate campus-based assessments for alignment to the standards and curriculum and revise where appropriate.
d. Offer after-school tutorials for students who are falling behind.

83. A school leader requests that teachers identify exemplary student work in PLCs and post the student work in their classrooms. The school leader regularly visits classrooms to view and evaluate the work that is posted. Which of the following best explains why the school leader made this request?

a. The school leader desires to be involved in analyzing student work.
b. The school leader is encouraging teacher collaboration.
c. The school leader is enforcing adherence to the standards-based curriculum.
d. The school leader believes that all students should be recognized for their performance.

84. A school leader would like to increase the use of differentiated instruction as an instructional strategy on campus. Which of the following actions would be most effective in achieving this goal?

a. Publicly recognize teachers who use differentiated instruction in the classroom.
b. Purchase books about differentiated instruction and distribute them to all of the teachers.
c. Model differentiated instruction during professional development sessions and monitor classroom implementation.
d. Hire an instructional coach that can train teachers how to use differentiated instruction in the classroom and evaluate their efficacy.

85. Which of the following activities would not be evidence that all students are being prepared for and have access to a challenging curriculum?

a. Students who were enrolled in pre-advanced placement courses in middle school are automatically enrolled in advanced placement courses in high school.
b. The school leader regular monitors student performance data on tests and in classes to determine alignment of campus-based assessment to standardized assessment.
c. All students are administered college entrance exams on the school campus at no cost to the student.
d. Students who have a history of meeting satisfactory performance standards on standardized tests are offered enrichment courses to help them reach mastery performance levels.

86. The leadership team of an elementary school has implemented a new math software program for all students in grades three through five. After three months of using the program, the students participated in a district benchmark exam and they showed little to no growth in math performance overall. What step should the leadership team take next?

a. Abandon the program because it is not effective.
b. Develop a plan for monitoring the math program at shorter intervals to determine its efficacy.
c. Reduce the number of students using the math program.
d. Increase the amount of time that students use the program.

87. The math department is excited that for the third consecutive time, most of the seventh-grade students have earned perfect scores on their six-week report cards. The Dean of Instruction is concerned by this news and requests to examine student work samples and class grades. Which of the following is a likely reason that the dean is concerned?

a. The data may indicate that the students are not receiving rigorous curriculum and instruction.
b. The math department's performance may have misinterpreted the student data.
c. The few students who did not receive perfect grades may be falling behind.
d. The students are likely committing acts of academic dishonesty.

88. The school principal had a meeting unexpectedly be cancelled and decided to use the free time to engage in activities on campus related to curriculum and instruction. Which of the following activities should the principal choose to engage in?

a. Assist with lunch duty.
b. Identify students to tutor in a small group.
c. Visit professional learning committees to engage in discussion regarding student progress.
d. Analyze student performance data from the most recent benchmark assessment.

89. A newly appointed principal has been advised that the teachers on campus are disgruntled and resistant to change. Which of the following is the best action for the principal to take first to address this issue?

a. Send out a survey to all teachers to assess campus culture.
b. Meet with a focus group of teacher leaders and allow them to voice their concerns.
c. Hold an all-staff meeting and communicate the vision for the school.
d. Send an email to all teachers informing them of new policies and procedures.

90. Which of the following is the best example of a school leader providing a safe environment for teacher to express their beliefs and ideas?

a. Scheduling monthly one-on-one meetings with individual teachers.
b. Placing a suggestion box in the teachers' lounge.
c. Administering an electronic survey to campus staff to obtain feedback.
d. Providing collaborative meeting time for teachers and meeting with them regularly to discuss their ideas.

91. A middle school principal decides to select and train several lead teachers in the math department to conduct action research on campus. This decision is an example of which of the following strategies?

a. Providing teachers with the opportunity to take appropriate risks for improving teaching and learning.
b. Encouraging collaboration between teachers to support professional growth.
c. Using data-driven decision making to improve student performance.
d. Giving teachers voice in school decisions.

92. XYZ school district requires a minimum number of professional development hours to be completed by teachers employed in the district annually. A high school principal notices that each year, teachers have difficulty meeting this expectation and look for last minute professional development opportunities at the end of the school year. What action might the principal take to address this issue?

a. Personally deliver professional development sessions to staff monthly.
b. Allocate more money in the budget to professional development.
c. Monitor professional development activities more frequently throughout the school year.
d. Provide incentives to teachers who complete all of their professional development activities at the beginning of the school year.

93. Which of the following is a primary benefit of professional learning communities?

a. To provide opportunities for teachers to share ideas.
b. To provide constructive feedback on student performance.
c. To identify areas in the curriculum that need revision.
d. To ensure that the standards-based curriculum is delivered.

94. The Dean of Instruction of a 9th grade high school academy would like to monitor student progress for the grading period. Which of the following sources of data would best inform the dean of student progress?

a. Student portfolios of work samples from previous and current marking periods.
b. Benchmark scores from the previous and current marking periods.
c. Anecdotal teacher notes.
d. Report card grades for the marking period.

95. The school principal institutes a professional learning community made up of social studies and reading teachers from grades 6th through 8th. This professional learning community is an example of which of the following?

a. Horizontal alignment of curriculum and instruction.
b. Vertical alignment of curriculum and instruction.
c. Horizontal and vertical alignment of curriculum and instruction.
d. Cross-cultural integration of curriculum and instruction.

96. A principal notices that even though teachers actively participate in professional development throughout the school year, there seems to be little evidence of changes in instructional practices on campus. Which of the following questions best addresses the concern of the principal?

a. What is the process for giving feedback on the efficacy of professional development offered to teachers?
b. Are professional development sessions aligned to the curriculum, instruction, and programs of this campus?
c. How much does professional development impact the school budget?
d. How can I make time in my schedule to attend professional development sessions with the teachers?

97. Which of the following sources and types of data would be best to use to provide feedback to teachers so that they can improve student learning?

a. Classroom observations, student class grades, and summative assessment data.
b. Formative assessment data, attendance data, and behavior data.
c. Classroom observations, survey data, and diagnostic testing data.
d. Formative assessment data, diagnostic testing data, and projected performance data.

98. Staff morale at ABC Elementary school is very low and is impacting staff and student performance. Which of the following steps should the principal take first to repair staff morale?

a. Host an all-staff pep rally to encourage everyone.
b. Create a committee to advise the principal on how to repair staff morale.
c. Buy gifts for the staff.
d. Administer a survey to identify the causes of low morale.

99. Other than classroom observations, which of the following would best provide an additional source of data for teacher evaluation?

a. Student performance data.
b. Student surveys.
c. Parent surveys.
d. Teacher self-assessments.

100. A school leader is faced with an impending budget cut for the upcoming school year. When deciding how to reallocate funds, which of the following strategies should the school leader implement?

a. Identify the most expensive budget items and reduce their allocations.
b. Identify the least expensive budget items and eliminate them.
c. Prioritize budget items that most closely align to the school goals.
d. Apply for grants to replace the lost funds.

Constructed Response

1. As a school leader who avidly pursues your own professional development (PD), you have read research statistics showing the high rate of attrition among new teachers, many of whom resign before even completing their probationary periods. This trend is apparent in your school as well. Although your school sponsors in-service trainings, and new teachers are assigned mentors when available while lead teachers double as mentors in other instances, you feel PD is not systematic enough, does not motivate teachers or guide new teachers enough, and is not really data-driven. You want to make it more effective to retain new teachers and improve faculty expertise in the interest of better student learning outcomes.

Write an approximately 150-300-word document to obtain new teacher feedback about their induction needs; experienced teacher feedback about their ongoing PD needs; and experienced teacher and teacher leader input for organizing more effective mentoring, coaching, and training. Include the following:

- Clarify for all recipients how their individual and collective perspectives can contribute to improving student outcomes by improving teaching quality.
- Describe one issue essential for consideration in designing, planning, and implementing new PD programs and strategies.
- Identify one kind of data or information that would best inform the design, planning, and implementation of new PD initiatives.
- Explain how the data or information you identified would be of use in improving the professional development activities at your school.

2. A group of students who identify with the LGBTQ community has approached you, their high school principal, to voice concerns that their interests are not addressed in the school curriculum. They want more content and activities relevant to their sexual and gender identities and the challenges they face interacting with society. Moreover, they believe adding such content could promote understanding among the student body, which in turn would mitigate bullying and harassment. Your school has progressively innovated to include student representatives on several committees, including a curriculum committee, anti-bullying committee, and student support committee.

Write an approximately 150-300-word proposal to all relevant committees, school leadership teams, administrators, faculty, and others as appropriate for incorporating content relevant to students who identify with the LGBTQ community and issues into the curriculum. Include the following:

- Depict one major issue for consideration in identifying, designing, and planning this addition to the curriculum.
- Explain what kinds of impacts the issue you depicted could have on how well the school will be able to implement this curricular addition.
- Specify one kind of information or data that you and collaborating staff and students could most use to help identify, design, and plan applicable curriculum content.
- Explain how the kind of information or data you specified would help with the curriculum design and planning.

3. You are a principal of a middle school where school psychologists have trained faculty and staff in administering individual programs of tiered positive behavior interventions and supports, small-group instruction, and intensive individualized interventions for a small percentage of students displaying problem behaviors. These have been very successful, not only according to staff reports, but also as proven by student data. Now you want to initiate a school-wide tiered positive behavior support program of prevention and intervention. Based on the individual successes, you have ample staff support and no resistance to the concept of a school-wide positive behavior support system. However, many staff members are concerned how the implementation process will affect daily management of school operations during the transitional period.

- Write an approximately 150-300-word proposal to school administrators, faculty, school psychologists, social workers, and other staff about the rationale for and benefits of implementing a school-wide behavior support system. Include the following: Describe one issue you find most central to consider for implementing the tiered prevention and intervention support model on a school-wide basis.
- Identify at least one step that the school could take to facilitate the implementation of a school-wide behavior support system.
- Explain how the step you identified would make implementation of the behavior management system throughout the school more practicable and successful.

Answer Key and Explanations for Test #2

Multiple Choice Questions

1. D: School leaders should use both quantitative and qualitative data to inform the school vision, mission, and goals. Assessment data and grades are important data points, but of the options provided, combining data from assessments and from stakeholder feedback would provide the most comprehensive data for a school leader. Formative assessment may include course grades, benchmark exams, and other data points. Summative assessments may include standardized tests or campus-based exams for credit or matriculation.

2. C: Diverse students are frequently overrepresented in special education due to inadequate educator knowledge and/or preparation for distinguishing such differences vs. true disabilities affecting learning and performance. School leaders address this inequity best by analyzing assessment instruments used to evaluate students for special education—which often require accommodations, modifications, or replacement with alternative assessments for diverse learners—rather than grade-level placement procedures because these students need instruction enabling them to perform at grade level, special education teaching strategies, or special curriculum and expectations, all of which are after the fact.

3. B: Change in temperament or evasion of work, such as through frequent unexplained absences, are very strong indicators of a staff member who is stressed or feeling overwhelmed, or is experiencing personal challenges. A change in work quality for a short term could be circumstantial, but over long periods of time, a decline in work quality could be an indicator of other factors such as mental health and stress. The school leader should recommend that the staff member take advantage of mental health and counseling resources that are available while respecting the staff member's privacy.

4. B: Researchers found that, among public schools, those with higher performance than others each seemed to have a unique combination of factors contributing to their success. These factors include having a clear and shared focus, having high expectations and standards for students, and high levels of family and community involvement. An effective school leader is a significant factor in high performing schools but is not the only determinant of success. Similarly, alignment of curriculum and instruction and frequent monitoring of teaching and learning are critical success factors but cannot be deemed the most important. Finally, school need resources for success, but many public schools have demonstrated success with meager funding.

5. C: The school board elects or hires and supervises the superintendent, who in turns hires and supervises the school principal. In the hierarchy of public education leadership, the school board makes policy decisions based on state and local legislature and the superintendent implements these policies. School principals apply these policies to the daily operations of the school. There may be instances in which a principal participates in a school board meeting, such as by reporting data or speaking, but these activities are not part of the regular responsibilities of a principal in relation to the school board.

6. C: School leaders should frequently highlight successes related to accomplishing the school vision to show stakeholders that the vision is viable and successful. Ceremonies for celebrating successes and other ways of highlighting successes are beneficial but must be conducted frequently in order to change a negative school culture. Providing professional development for teachers related to culture can be beneficial but would not address issues with culture for all employees on campus. Additionally, it is important for leaders to make observations about school culture, but observations without action will not positively impact school culture.

7. D: Educators should base their education practices on research-based practices with proven results. These practices are outlined in peer-reviewed research and texts based on this type of research. Additionally, the Department of Education reports on the efficacy of educational programs, products, practices, and policies through the What Works Clearinghouse. Educators should prioritize educational practices that have been proven to be effective before implementing practices based on personal experience or experimentation that is often a component of action research.

8. B: While staying informed of new trends and technology is useful in this role, it is not central to the actual implementation of a new technology that is in its early implementation. Change management often requires more direct support of a wide range of needs from staff and students. Demonstrating the use of the technology (choice A), setting expectations and encouraging effort (choice C), and helping with implementation (choice D) all are a more direct way the school leader should help to implement change in this situation.

9. A: Before engaging any community resource, school leaders must consider whether it is compatible with the school's vision and mission. Some resources may have impact in the long-term rather than immediately and should not be discarded because effects will not be seen immediately. Additionally, as communities develop, new resources may be made available. Not all available resources will have a history of prior implementation but may prove beneficial for student learning. Similarly, as the school builds new partnerships, community resources may become available through new and emerging community relationships.

10. C: To encourage teacher leadership, school leaders must create safe environments wherein teachers can take risks and think creatively. School leaders should share authority with teachers to assist them in developing leadership skills and demonstrate responsibility. Increasing a teacher's workload with work that is not directly related to increased responsibilities or to skill refinement is not an example of developing a teacher. Additionally, leaders must differentiate support for teachers based on the current performance, skill, and attitudes.

11. D: According to some school consensus-building models, although the ideal is for 100 percent of faculty members to agree to implement a recommendation, this is not always realistic and is not required 100 percent of the time. If consensus seems impossible, many schools have a rule stating that 80 percent of members agreeing is sufficient; dissenting members must promise not only to refrain from obstructing implementation, but furthermore to support it.

12. B: Students having family issues, or personal problems whose treatment involves family, are referred to family counselors. Group counseling promotes social skills and healthy interaction and can be provided within the school environment when the groups are selected with intention. Career counselors can help students choose career paths and preparation. Career counseling is often performed in schools by guidance counselors and others, making referrals infrequent.

13. B: Campus-based personnel are dedicated to the campus and work under the direct supervision of the campus principal. District personnel are supervised by other district personnel but provide services to campuses. In many public schools, transportation workers, food service workers, and psychologists are district personnel who provide services to more than one campus. However, in general, most school counselors are dedicated to one campus and are supervised by the school principal.

14. B: External stressors can create short-term or long-term obstacles for student learning and achievement and can lead to or be evidence of mental health issues. Not all student mental health issues or crises carry an official diagnosis; however, educators can provide support and resources for the symptoms that students display. Furthermore, students with diagnosed mental health issues may be provided support and resources through a 504-education plan in addition to or in lieu of an individualized education plan. Additionally, educators can offer resources and support to students with mental health issues who do not receive services under either program.

15. B: Hosting a community meeting to communicate the school vision pertains to the implementation stages of vision and goals, not the development and planning stage. In order to create a shared vision, the school leader should make the vision relevant to the community, solicit community input, and based the vision and goals on data. After the vision has been developed with the community in mind, the vision can be shared with others.

16. D: Learning objectives are not what educators hope to accomplish, want to teach students, or what students expect teachers to impart to them. Instead, they are what educators expect their students to be able to do after they have instructed them in a content subject lesson, unit, or course. Experts observe that a common teacher error is to misinterpret learning objectives as things they plan to do during instruction instead of what they will expect students to do following instruction.

17. A: Individual students have different learning styles, skills, strengths, and weaknesses, so it is important to administer multiple and varied assessments to assemble as comprehensive a picture as possible of each student's existing knowledge, new learning, and instructional needs. Multiple assessments are not used to keep students from forgetting. Summative assessments following instruction are not sufficient as they do not continuously assess student learning and progress, and they do not enable teachers to adjust ongoing instruction to be more effective as formative assessments made during instruction do.

18. C: Staff growth though professional development is important. When identifying professional development for staff members, school leaders should consider school goals as well as individual goals of staff members. This will ensure that staff members are equipped to contribute to achieving school goals but also grow in areas that they have established personal goals.

19. B: Research finds that school leader participation in PD is what determines teacher and school-wide participation in PD. School leaders set an example for teachers by actively engaging in the PD that teachers are expected to engage in. School leaders should have a vision for PD offerings but can empower teachers to choose PD offerings that meet their needs. School leaders can facilitate PD activities but should also allow teacher leaders to facilitate PD as well. School leaders should monitor implementation of PD but this activity is not directly related to being a role model for teachers.

20. A: Implementing differentiated instruction helps teachers to meet students where they are based on performance, learning style, and other student characteristics. Instruction can be differentiated based on lesson delivery, student activities, and student assessment. However, standards are often standardized and must remain the same for students as all students are expected to learn and succeed. Teachers can provide individualized resources and support to help students to meet those needs.

21. C: Students designing digital storybooks is the best example of creating content using digital media. It is beneficial for students to access information using technology, such as visiting wiki pages. Students can also curate content that already exists, such as gathering photos from the web.

However, creating content using digital media empowers students to use technology at the highest level of Bloom's taxonomy.

22. A: Classroom management systems, e.g., tiered school-wide positive behavior support systems, make learning environments orderly, enabling students to learn more easily and succeed academically. Rather than only controlling student behavior, they foster and sustain appropriate classroom behavior while also promoting student emotional and social development. They are effective for increasing both prosocial behavior and academic engagement in students. By providing universal supports in the first-tier school-wide, they succeed for 80-85 percent of students, while individualized intensive interventions are reserved for the remaining 15-20 percent in the third tier.

23. A: According to some education experts (cf. WestEd.org), school principals and districts surveyed across the United States have reported generally positive impressions of standards-based accountability systems, saying these have improved curriculum and instruction, student assessment practices (c), and student expectations and achievement. However, many districts (over 40 percent) also reported that teacher morale had been adversely affected by accountability pressures.

24. A: According to the New Teacher Project (2011), design standards for effective teacher evaluation systems include evaluating teachers a minimum of yearly, using multiple levels (four or five) for rating teachers, basing evaluations on clear instructional excellence standards prioritizing student learning, using multiple performance measures emphasizing teacher impact on student academic progress, making frequent observations and giving critical and/or constructive feedback, and making evaluation outcomes significant by using them as a major factor in important teacher employment decisions.

25. D: When planning for differentiated instruction, teachers should utilize as much data as possible that can be useful in determining how students can best learn. Identification in special populations such as special education, English as second language, gifted and talented, and others are helpful when planning differentiated instruction but are not the only factors to be considered. Student interests, learning styles, formative and summative data, and other relevant data should all be considered when planning differentiated instruction.

26. A: Formative data helps teachers to assess their effectiveness during instruction (rather than after) and accordingly make adjustments to improve student outcomes. Summative data can assist teachers in identifying areas of improvement in their teaching practice but is often too late to identify specific remedial student groups. Student profiles from permanent records (e.g., demographics, assessment histories, family information, etc.) give less detailed information provide less information to inform instruction. Enrollment data helps educators identify budgetary needs and student demographic distributions, but do not inform instruction, staff development, remedial student groups, or information plans.

27. C: According to principles of adult learning, adults learn best in more informal formats rather than how children learn by following a formal curriculum. They prefer guidance and choices rather than directive instruction. Both children and adults learn by doing, but active, hands-on participation is even more important for adult learning. Adults want to learn practical information they need and can use immediately in their work rather than theoretical concepts.

28. B: Effective induction programs offered by the New Teacher Center and others have impacts on schools of making new teachers more effective, increasing teacher retention rates, strengthening teacher leadership, addressing education inequities, *and* increasing student learning and achievement.

29. D: School principals should remain objective when observing teachers, regardless of their tenure or contract status. An evaluation rubric for teacher assessment should be used fairly and objectively for all teachers. A principal should observe what assignments the teacher gives the students, whether they are actively implementing new strategies, and the overall classroom environment and culture.

30. A: A school leader should evaluate technology data systems used in the school by how well they provide relevant data for decision making. Affordability and whether other schools are using the data system are important questions to ask when considering purchasing a data system but are less relevant when evaluating the system after use. User friendliness is not as important in evaluation if training and support are readily available to staff who will use the data system.

31. D: To help students prepare for their futures, high schools should design curricula relevant to students' lives, communities, and cultural milieus. This includes the career and technical education they will need for today's world, which public high schools must offer. School partnerships with colleges and universities best prepare students for higher education, while community-based and project-based learning best prepare students for employment.

32. C: The US Department of Justice (DOJ) collaborated with the US Department of Education (ED) in producing a positive school discipline guidance package as part of the SSDI to prevent or reduce student movement from schools to justice and correctional systems, not match school discipline to practices in those systems; replace disciplinary exclusion with better alternatives, rather than regard student justice involvement as inevitable and wait to address that; ensure Titles IV and VI of the Civil Rights Act prohibiting discrimination are enforced, which is the DOJ's job; and establish fair disciplinary practices to keep all students in school, not exclude any.

33. B: Establishing an anti-discrimination policy helps all staff and students to understand the regulations relating to bias and discrimination on campus. Describing what constitutes bias and discrimination makes it easier to identify violations on campus. Additionally, establishing a committee that is focused on cultural awareness and inclusion can help to decrease educational and institutional bias and discriminatory practices. Establishing and enforcing rules as limited efficacy if there is limited understanding of the rationale behind the rules. Having a culturally diverse staff is beneficially, but persons of underrepresented cultures should not be required to teach others about their cultures if they do not choose to. It is beneficial to include opportunities for students to learn about other cultures in the classroom, however this strategy does help to identify bias and discriminatory practices on campus.

34. D: Behavioral codes of conduct govern student, faculty, staff, and visitor behavior in schools. State regulations typically require schools to give teachers copies upon adoption, send all parents summaries before school years start, and give students copies when school years begin. However, to gain stakeholder buy in and to assure collective understanding and agreement, conduct codes can be developed jointly by parents, teachers, and students.

35. A: Research shows that, among others, one reason schools should collaborate with their communities to provide mental health services is that schools are not suitable settings for clinical psychiatric care and similar services. When collaborating with communities, school staff must work not only with families and community service providers, but also with policymakers to coordinate and connect needed support processes. A cohesive and integrated mental health intervention continuum must address *both* severe student problems *and* universal student needs.

36. B: Change is often opposed when stakeholders feel that the change is done without their consent and is outside of their control. As a result, obtaining stakeholder buy in can help make changes more effective. Goals should align to the changes but this strategy by itself will not help to manage the change. Additional training will be ineffective if stakeholders are opposed to the change. School leaders should listen to those who are opposed to the change and attempt to address their concerns rather than removing them from campus.

37. A: School-wide positive behavior support programs typically have three tiers. In tier 1, all students receive universal instructional and behavioral supports and interventions, which are effective for the majority. In tier 2, a minority of students needing more behavior support receive small-group instruction in academic subjects and emotional and social skills. In tier 3, an even smaller minority not responding to tier 2 interventions receives intensive, individualized interventions.

38. C: According to the Collaborative for Academic, Social, and Emotional Learning (CASEL), effective SEL programs incorporate sequenced and systematic programming across all grade levels, monitor the programming continuously, offer opportunities for students to practice the skills they learn, and coordinate school environments with community environments.

39. D: Because research studies repeatedly prove student benefits of smaller class sizes, school leaders must hire and retain adequate *human* resources in terms of quantity and quality. For a safe, comfortable teaching and learning environment, school leaders must provide adequate *physical* resources like space, furniture, lighting, temperature control, etc. They must manage *fiscal* resources well to manage *all* other resources, not just some.

40. A: Data showing school improvement goals that are behind schedule indicate a need to update the school improvement plan—either by adjusting completion time criteria if school leaders and staff determine they were unrealistic in either case, or by adjusting instruction to be more effective if they determine current methods are delaying progress.

41. C: Researchers have identified a number of transformational school leader practices promoting organizational staff learning, including demonstrating their high expectations not only for students to learn and achieve, but equally for teachers to be innovative and effective; modeling ongoing learning in their own practices and affording staff opportunities to learn from one another. These leaders also encourage staff to research, learn, and reflect independently.

42. B: According to researchers (Mitchell and Sackney, 1998), both reflection (i.e., considering their own practices) and conversation (i.e., discussing their and colleagues' practices) enable teachers to have awareness of their own and others' practices, evaluate them, and discover possible alternatives. These are cognitive processes. Affirmation of one another as professionals, and invitation into school decision-making both validate all staff members' contributions, acknowledge individual professional competencies, and thereby establish positive working relationships. These are affective processes.

43. B: Research finds the relationship between school leadership and student outcomes is indirect rather than direct. Rather than motivating student achievement directly, effective school leadership promotes a school climate conducive to learning. Substantial research has demonstrated that there is a relationship between school leadership and student outcomes, although the relationship is indirect.

44. D: Effective new teacher induction programs should focus on supporting not only the new teachers, but also the school leaders who guide them. This requires offering professional development not only to new teachers, but equally to their mentors, school leaders, and other site leaders. Effective induction programs use research-based and standards-based assessment instruments to assess and inform new teacher performance. The ultimate goal of teacher induction programs that make teachers more effective is to improve student achievement.

45. C: For school professional development to meet student needs and achieve school goals best, it should be provided to *all* staff, not only to teachers, specialists, and other faculty or professionals. It should also be embedded in the job rather than separated, differentiated to address the individual challenge areas of teachers and other staff members, and provided on an ongoing basis instead of a periodic one.

46. B: Research from Stanford University (Grissom, Loeb, and Master, 2013) into effective school leader use of instructional time finds that improvements in student achievement are predicted by time spent on evaluation of teachers and/or curriculum, coaching teachers, and developing the school education program. It is *not* predicted in informal classroom walkthroughs, particularly in high schools. The investigators speculate this may be because school leaders frequently do not incorporate walkthroughs into broader strategies for school improvement.

47. A: To realize instructional change over time, professional development (PD) must be provided on an ongoing basis and reinforced through repetition and classroom follow-up activities. Teachers need theoretical understanding not only of the theory underling instructional practices, but also of how they can apply theory to practice. PD is best administered as a component of a comprehensive, systematic, district-supported educational reform process. When school leaders furnish PD, they should be careful to avoid topics lacking research support, unrelated to student learning, and popular new fads.

48. C: Parents and other community members must demand and support quality professional development (PD) that improves teaching, school leadership, and student achievement. School boards must hold educators accountable for results and provide policies clarifying that the purpose of PD is to enhance educator efficacy and thus student learning. Educators who organize and facilitate PD must understand which student learning needs they and their fellow educators have difficulty addressing. School system administrators must allot time and otherwise facilitate PD that will help educators address student learning problems.

49. D: If the Individualized Education Program (IEP) committee determines a student's behavior was a manifestation of their disability, the school cannot expel the student or apply the same disciplinary procedures indicated for students without disabilities. The IEP committee's plan will address any or all of these areas: ensuring the IEP is consistently implemented as it is written; changing the IEP to include accommodations, services, etc. as needed; further evaluations to identify additional services that may be needed; and/or functional behavior assessment to inform interventions.

50. B: School leaders and district personnel can usually project employee salaries for the next school year fairly easily, but it is more difficult to predict healthcare or other employee benefits. Although transportation expenses are essential, they are *not* included in school budgets. Not only are regular school buses and drivers expensive, individual transportation plans included in special education students' Individualized Education Program (IEPs) are even more so, and furnishing homeless and/or other students with transportation is yet another expense. In addition, school district planners *must* reserve some amount of the budget for unexpected emergency school facility repairs, etc.

51. A: According to the American Association of School Administrators (AASA) Center for System Leadership, applying systems thinking to school reform results in, among other things, continuous improvement of school system policies and practices, curriculum aligned system-wide, school system interconnection with other community systems, and priorities identified (and resources allocated accordingly) for *universal* student success.

52. A: Experts have identified four purposes of school technology use: as a productivity tool for applying application software to solve problems, manage information, and create sophisticated products; as information access and communications enhancement via the Internet and associated information technologies; as a cognitive stimulus by giving students real-life experiences and authentic simulations to extend learning and stimulate cognitive development; and as instructional content by employing ever more advanced digital content for teaching, drilling, and practicing.

53. B: Experts believe that every school leader is motivated to conduct good teacher evaluations. However, they find one of the most important factors is whether school leaders make time to observe teachers regularly and frequently, even if only briefly each time. They emphasize that school leaders must evaluate teachers in a continuous process rather than a series of isolated events.

54. D: Researchers have found that, in more effective schools, novice teachers are assigned students with similar average achievement as students assigned to more experienced teachers; in other words, more effective schools and leaders assign classes more equitably to novice teachers than less effective schools do. More effective schools and leaders do not assign lower-achieving or higher-achieving students to novice teachers, nor do they assign them randomly relative to student achievement.

55. D: Reducing the teachers' teaching styles is not a priority as long as the teacher is effective at achieving standards in the curriculum. Reducing variability in classrooms throughout the school tends to promote efficiency in purchasing, and in producing testing materials, since each department can use the same materials. This also could allow for benchmarking from class to class, which helps with pacing the curriculum throughout the year. Other procedures and policies, such as bathroom policies or electronic device policies can promote safety by making sure each student is accounted for.

56. C: School leaders must assure most that the specific responsibilities of each member of the command and control group are clearly defined, including for a variety of different crisis situations, in advance. Tenure is not an equitable way of selecting members. Distributing leadership could cause confusion during a crisis, and a complex reporting system could defeat the whole purpose of such a team.

57. A: To be effective, research finds tiered behavior management systems applied at the classroom level should be established early in the school year; however, individual programs for disruptive student behaviors may begin at any time as needed. Classroom behavior management systems should be applied across the grades to give students consistent, ongoing input and reinforcement of procedures, rules, and expectations; and throughout the school year without fading to reinforce and support positive behavior.

58. C: Among many others, NASSP recommendations for promoting student mental health (MH) include providing comprehensive staff development\not only to school employees, but also to community service personnel working in the school; training school and community staff working in the school in promoting school-wide positive environments, which is found effective; training school staff in using referral mechanisms to help students access community MH services; and training both school and community staff working in schools in early identification of MH disorders and risks for these.

59. B: The NSBA acknowledges that school districts ARE committed to giving students healthy nutrition. However, it also points out that many school districts, already underfunded, cannot afford the additional expense of meeting the law's stricter nutrition standards as written—particularly because many of its regulations are *not* funded. Students are going hungry not because the regulations limit food amounts, but because they dislike the food, do not eat it, and so it goes wasted.

60. B: The majority of female staffs' perception of the supervisor's nicknames as inoffensive could indicate he does not consciously intend disrespect by using them and also suggests a positive relationship between staff and principal. Therefore, reprimanding the supervisor and asking for a public apology is not most appropriate. However, her complaint must be acknowledged and not discredited simply for lack of agreement. As the supervisor's address may not constitute sexual harassment and most staff members do not perceive it as such, a meeting to review laws is also not the best action. The principal should make the supervisor aware of how his habit is perceived by some and that he needs to cease referring to female employees in this manner. School leaders must also defer to policies and procedures outlined by their school board and district regarding sexual harassment, including policies on documentation and reporting.

61. C: To realize their school goals for students despite economic constraints, instead of the common but counterproductive school reactions of postponing improvements or cutting services and programs students need, school leaders can identify programs that are expensive but do not improve student performance while considering different alternatives for achieving the same results, like providing professional development *less* expensively by implementing study groups instead of paying for guest speakers and workshops.

62. C: Most school expenditures are related to classroom instruction. These expenditures include teacher salaries, libraries, professional development for teachers, curriculum development, and instructional technology. Operations is the next highest percentage of budgetary expenditures, followed by administration and student support services. Student support services involves expenses such as social work, guidance, health expenses, and psychological services.

63. D: School leaders are responsible for knowing *and* enforcing student and parent rights to privacy and confidentiality of educational records under the Family Educational Rights and Privacy Act (FERPA) and Individuals with Disabilities Education Act (IDEA). They must know and understand exceptions to these laws, which can require them to disclose student records to law enforcement and others. School leaders are responsible for both disclosing information to third parties *and* obtaining the written parental consent required for such disclosures. They are also responsible for creating policy governing access to student records by parties other than parents and eligible students.

64. C: Although the fundamental American right to information access is important, it is not the only or most important factor in school acceptable use policies (AUPs). Some school districts require student agreement and parental permission forms for minor (under 18) students for independent electronic information use, but this is not always the case. Student intellectual freedom depends on their responsibility for accepting limits in that freedom. Experts do advise schools to contact electronic freedom of information organizations to inform themselves fully.

65. B: The school leader should *initially* ensure that district resources allocated for the school ELL program are sufficient to meet federal and state program requirements. Basing calculations on the previous fiscal year will not account for changes in the coming year. Basing ELL program resources on the remainder left after allocating the rest to maintain current funding for other programs will not necessarily or likely ensure sufficient funds to meet legal mandates for the ELL program. Evaluating program effectiveness is a later step during and following program administration.

66. B: Hazard analysis: analyzing food service operation, determining likely food safety hazards and control measures. Identifying CCPs: identifying those few control measures absolutely essential to food safety. Determining critical limits: cooking temperatures, times, and other observable and measurable safety-defining boundaries. Establishing CCP monitoring procedures: tracking CCP control as food flows through operations. Planning corrective actions: planning what to do when a critical limit at a CCP is not met and communicating to and training employees in preventive decisions. Verification procedures: ensuring a scientifically sound system for effective hazard control. Record-keeping system: documenting the HACCP system and plan.

67. C: Narrative writing tells a story. School leaders need narrative writing skills to relate school success stories. They need persuasive writing skills to convince others to agree with the positions they take, opinions they express, and actions they propose. They might use descriptive writing skills to paint vivid pictures for readers of school activities and situations. They need expository writing skills for informing their readers of facts, statistics, plans, procedures, and other objective information.

68. A: Lack of family and community involvement is typically not a result of parents and others being uninterested in students' learning, working with educators, or influencing students' futures. It is more likely the result of unrealistic educator attitudes in expecting parents and others to seek involvement independently, and some educator methods are ineffective, like posting fliers at school when parents rarely visit, sending them home with students who forget to give them to parents, etc. Experts find educator efforts must be more intensive and organized to involve families and communities.

69. D: Studies find that, regardless of culture, ethnicity, income, or race, diverse families overall tend to have very similar high aspirations and expectations for their children, care about their success similarly, and (within their means) share similar active involvement in their children's educations.

70. D: Schools and communities benefit mutually from school leader outreach. For example, community partners become better informed about school functions and needs *and* develop a sense of ownership in the school. They appreciate and remember the invitations, acknowledgements, and thanks of school leaders. School leaders show they recognize their school belongs to the community by offering community access to school facilities for various events, benefiting not only the community but also the school when community members gain better understandings of the school and its positive effects on student lives.

71. A: Vision and goals are deemed appropriate when they are based on multiple sources of data that reflect current practice. It is important for school leaders to solicit buy in from community members, but this is not an indicator of the appropriateness of the goals. Additionally, the school vision and goals can leverage school strengths, but areas of deficit or weakness are often addressed the goals. Although schools may have similar demographics and performance history, the school vision and goals should be based upon a thorough analysis of the data unique to the campus. Consequently, the vision and goals of schools may differ even though the performance history and demographics of the school may appear to be similar.

72. C: When developing a vision and goals for the school, the school leader must ensure that the vision and goals align with the local, state, and federal policies. Local, state, and federal policies include curriculum and assessment standards that must be adhered to. The school leader must determine whether the focus on a fine arts program would assist the school in meeting these standards. If not, it would not be appropriate to include the fine arts program in the school vision and goals. The number of students currently participating in the program is not relevant to the determination. Additionally, the assessment of human and fiscal resources occurs after the vision and goals have been developed.

73. C: Buy in from internal and external community members would be the most likely strategy for engaging stakeholders in the implementation of the school vision and goals. Buy in is achieved when stakeholders are included in the process of developing the school vision and goals. When stakeholders are part of the process, they are more likely to feel ownership of the product which motivates them to engage in implementation. Communicating the school vision and goals to the community is important, but it may not lead to engagement in implementation if stakeholders do not feel that they were including in the process of developing the vision and goals.

74. A: A school leader must develop a plan for assessing and monitoring progress toward established goals. When monitoring is done consistently, the school leader will be aware of whether the school is meeting, exceeding, or falling short of established goals in a timely manner. Regularly monitoring of progress toward goals will allow the school leader opportunity to make corrections in the strategies and actions that are implemented, if needed.

75. B: Given that students were consistently performing well in math with the exception of three specific math objectives indicates that there is an issue with the curriculum being used to teach those objectives. Factors such as teacher quality or biased assessments would negatively impact student performance in all objectives, not just a select few and performance would vary from student to student. The most likely reason for students consistently underperforming in the same area despite being taught by different teachers is a misalignment of curriculum to the assessment of the objectives.

76. D: Student growth is the best data point to inform the principal as to whether the reading program was effective. An effective program would result in individual and collective student growth as measured by a pre- and post-assessment. Feedback from students and teachers is valuable and can be considered in the budgeting decision; however, a principal would not want to purchase a program if it does not produce results, even if the students and teachers viewed the program positively.

77. D: The most appropriate response that the principal can offer the PTO president is that the science curriculum purchase directly supports a school goal. All school resources such as curriculum should be aligned to the school vision and goals. Satisfactory student performance is not an appropriate response given that the school leader may have identified college preparation as an area of improvement, even if students were already meeting expectations in this area. Additionally, the cost of the curriculum is irrelevant if the curriculum is not aligned to the campus vision and goals.

78. B: Of the strategies listed, the strategy that best addresses the achievement gap is providing targeted interventions to students who perform unsatisfactorily. Disaggregating data helps to identify the achievement gap, but does not address it. Tracking and projecting student performance also has the potential to identify the achievement gap, but does not address it. Rather than lowering standards, holding high expectations and standards helps to reduce the achievement gap.

79. A: Teachers and staff have more buy in when changes are made if they are part of the process. Creating a committee that does not include school leadership demonstrates the leader's willingness to give authority to the staff to promote change and a willingness to accept changes that are not generated by leadership. Suggestion boxes and town hall meetings allow staff to share ideas, but these ideas still must be vetted by the school leader as a gate keeper and may not fully address the school's current culture. Teacher engagement in the Shared Decision-Making Committee is vital for school success, but will not likely address a campus-wide perception of top-down leadership.

80. C: Providing teachers with aggregated student data, even in regular intervals, will not likely improve teacher practice. School leaders must disaggregate data to help teachers identify the data that is reflective of their students and their instructional practice. Disaggregated data should also be analyzed in a collaborative process to help identify needs and generate solutions to address those needs.

81. B: The data suggests that the students need more rigorous instruction since they are performing well, but not demonstrating growth. Rigorous Standards-based curriculum can be delivered at an appropriate level of rigor so that students experience learning and demonstrate growth. Instructional delivery may include classes labeled as honors classes, pre-Advanced Placement, or Advanced Placement courses; however, classes do not have to be labeled in order for a teacher to increase the level of instruction in a classroom.

82. C: Evaluating and revising campus-based assessments to ensure alignment to standards demonstrates a commitment to school-wide rigorous instruction. Assessments should accurately measure the standards. Increasing the offering of advanced placement and dual credit courses supports rigorous curriculum for some students who qualify, but does not impact rigor school wide. Similarly, increasing participation in college entrance exams does not raise the rigor of instruction on campus, but encourages students to seek and prepare for college admittance.

83. A: Requesting that teachers identify student work and post it, then reviewing the posted work demonstrates that the school leader wants to be involved in analyzing student work. The posted work will provide the school leader with an assessment of student performance as well as what teachers consider to be exemplary work. This request does not directly encourage teacher collaboration as teachers could make autonomous decisions regarding their students' performance. Additionally, the request does not directly exemplify an assessment of alignment to standards. Finally, not all students are recognized, only students who performed in an exemplary manner.

84. D: Hiring a coach that can train teachers to use differentiated instruction and evaluate them for efficacy would be the most effective strategy for increasing the uses of differentiated instruction on campus. An instructional coach can provide individual and collective support and can monitor and encourage continuous implementation of the strategy. Praising teachers who implement differentiated instruction creates a positive climate but does not help teachers who do not know how to implement differentiated instruction to do so. Similarly, providing resources and modeling are not sufficient actions to take to increase the use of differentiated instruction if teachers do not know how to implement it or do not see the benefit in implementing the strategy.

85. A: Student placement in courses should be based on relevant data. Automatically enrolling students in advanced placement courses without reviewing data could result in students being placed in classes that are too rigorous while students who were not previously enrolled could miss an opportunity to be placed in a challenging course. School leaders should monitor student performance data, ensure rigor and alignment of curriculum, and provide campus-wide opportunities for students when possible. In order to provide all students with preparation for and access to a challenging curriculum, students should have opportunities for an appropriate level of rigorous instruction based on their current academic performance.

86. B: Despite the students not showing growth on the district benchmark test, there is no evidence of the program's efficacy or inefficacy. First, the time period may be too short to determine if the program is effective. Secondly, it is unknown if the program was intended to have a direct impact on student performance measured by the benchmark exam. To determine the program's efficacy going forward, the leadership team must develop a plan for data collection and analysis at regular intervals. Only then can the leadership team determine the programs efficacy and whether the program should continue to be implemented on campus.

87. A: All students receiving perfect scores for 18 consecutive weeks may be an indication that the students are not receiving rigorous curriculum and instruction. While there is an expectation for students to be successful in the classroom, there is low statistical likelihood that all students would perform perfectly over extended periods of time if they were receiving instruction at or above their level. Each student should receive a rigorous curriculum which means delivering instruction at an appropriate level of challenge in order to grow students academically.

88. C: The principal has expressed a desire to engage in activities related to curriculum and instruction; therefore, assisting with lunch duty would not be an option. Analyzing data is a beneficial activity but is only indirectly related to curriculum and instruction. Similarly, tutoring students one time in isolation would not be beneficial use of the principal's time. Instead, the principal should engage in professional learning communities with teachers to discuss the implementation of curriculum and the results.

89. B: The new principal is aware that the teachers on campus are not happy; therefore, it is best to talk to a small group of teachers to understand what issues that they have. Sending a survey out is a good strategy, but not necessarily a first step as the data collected may not thoroughly describe the issues that the teachers have, especially if teachers do not feel that they can be honest on the survey. Also, an all-staff meeting can quickly get out of control if outspoken staff persons have unaddressed issues. Sending an email is impersonal and not an advisable first step.

90. D: Teachers need opportunities to share their beliefs and ideas about teaching and learning with the school leader and with one another. Teachers must belief that they operate in an environment that allows them to be open and honest when examining their own beliefs and practices. Suggestion boxes and surveys are one-way communication tools that do not allow for peer discussion, although anonymity may help teachers feel comfortable giving honest feedback. Providing collaborative meeting time for teachers and meeting with them regularly gives teachers the opportunity to discuss their ideas with one another, but also gives them the opportunity to share their ideas with the school leader when they are comfortable.

91. A: Supporting teachers in conducting action research on campus is an example of giving them opportunities to take risks for improving teaching and learning. Action research allows the teacher to identify the area of improvement and hypothesize which actions or strategies may lead to improving the identified area. Action research allows teachers to problem solve using solutions that they have developed which gives them the opportunity to take risks.

92. C: The goal of professional development is to foster continuous improvement of teaching and learning. Professional development has limited applicability if it is all conducted at the beginning of the school year or at the end of the school year. The best action that the principal can take is to monitor professional development at regular intervals throughout the school year and to encourage teachers to take advantage of timely professional development that can impact their practice during the school year.

93. D: One of the foundations of a professional learning community is identifying the standards and curriculum that must be taught and ensuring that the curriculum is delivered effectively. A question that PLC members must ask is "What do we want students to learn?". Answering this question ensures that the standards-based curriculum is prioritized, and that formative and summative assessment is a reflection of the curriculum that is taught.

94. A: Data must be compared from one point in time to another to determine progress. Benchmark tests are typically used to assess objectives taught during a certain period and do not necessarily assess the same objectives from test to test; therefore, benchmark scores would not necessarily compare the same data to determine progress. Student portfolios from multiple marking periods would provide an assessment of authentic student performance over time and would be most helpful in determining student progress.

95. C: The PLC will include teachers in the same grade level in different subjects which is horizontal alignment. The PLC will also include teachers in different grade levels in the same subject which is vertical alignment. Consequently, this PLC is an example of both horizontal and vertical alignment of curriculum and instruction.

96. B: The principal should determine which professional development sessions that teachers are attending and whether those sessions are aligned to the curriculum, instruction, and programs on campus. The professional development sessions may be informative but may not be practically applicable to the campus if they are not aligned with campus goals. For example, if a teacher attends a professional development session on project-based learning, yet the campus does not implement nor support project-based learning, there will be little to no evidence of changes in instructional practice on campus as a result of attendance to that session.

97. A: Classroom observations, student class grades, and summative assessment data would be the best sources of data to provide feedback to teachers to improve student learning. Data sources for improving teaching and learning should include instructional delivery (classroom observations) and student performance outcomes. Both formative and summative assessment data can be used to determine student mastery of objectives and efficacy of instructional delivery.

98. D: The first step that a principal must take is to determine the causes of the low morale. Implementing solutions without understanding the causes may lead to wasted time and resources if the solutions do not address the perceived problems. The principal should collect data to identify the issues that staff may have on campus and then develop appropriate solutions.

99. A: Student performance data is a valuable source of data for determining teacher efficacy. Effective instruction should result in student academic growth and satisfactory performance. Survey data and self- assessments can inform support and professional development for teachers but are not as useful in teacher evaluations due to their qualitative and subjective nature.

100. C: The school budget should be in alignment with the school vision and goals. When facing a budget shortfall, a school leader must scrutinize the budget to determine which areas of spending will most directly impact the school goals. Areas that do not directly impact school goals can have reduced budget allocations or be eliminated entirely.

Constructed Response

1. Essay question graders commonly look for the following elements in a strong response: strong content knowledge, clear organization, and effective arguments or examples. Language and usage are not usually strictly graded, but can make a big impact on the clarity of your ideas.

Please use the provided rubric to make sure your response meets these common criteria. Try to have a friend or family member grade your response for you or take a break after writing your response and return to grade it with fresh eyes.

Constructed Response Rubric

Domain	Description
Content Knowledge	• The response directly addresses every part of the prompt. • The response demonstrates independent knowledge of the topic. • The response discusses the topic at an appropriate depth.
Organization	• The response introduces the topic, usually with a thesis statement or by restating the prompt. • The response directly addresses the prompt by providing a clear and concise answer or solution. • The answer or solution is supported by logical arguments or evidence. • The response restates the main idea in the conclusion.
Arguments and Examples	• The response provides a reasonable answer to the prompt. • The answer is supported by strong reasoning or evidence. • The response develops ideas logically and connects ideas to one another. • The reasoning and evidence provided act to support a unified main idea.
Language and Usage	• The response demonstrates effective use of grammar and uses varied sentence structure throughout the response. • The response demonstrates correct use of spelling, punctuation, and capitalization. • The response demonstrates strong and varied use of vocabulary relevant to the topic and appropriate for the intended audience.

2. Essay question graders commonly look for the following elements in a strong response: strong content knowledge, clear organization, and effective arguments or examples. Language and usage are not usually strictly graded, but can make a big impact on the clarity of your ideas.

Please use the provided rubric to make sure your response meets these common criteria. Try to have a friend or family member grade your response for you or take a break after writing your response and return to grade it with fresh eyes.

Constructed Response Rubric

Domain	Description
Content Knowledge	• The response directly addresses every part of the prompt. • The response demonstrates independent knowledge of the topic. • The response discusses the topic at an appropriate depth.
Organization	• The response introduces the topic, usually with a thesis statement or by restating the prompt. • The response directly addresses the prompt by providing a clear and concise answer or solution. • The answer or solution is supported by logical arguments or evidence. • The response restates the main idea in the conclusion.
Arguments and Examples	• The response provides a reasonable answer to the prompt. • The answer is supported by strong reasoning or evidence. • The response develops ideas logically and connects ideas to one another. • The reasoning and evidence provided act to support a unified main idea.
Language and Usage	• The response demonstrates effective use of grammar and uses varied sentence structure throughout the response. • The response demonstrates correct use of spelling, punctuation, and capitalization. • The response demonstrates strong and varied use of vocabulary relevant to the topic and appropriate for the intended audience.

3. Essay question graders commonly look for the following elements in a strong response: strong content knowledge, clear organization, and effective arguments or examples. Language and usage are not usually strictly graded, but can make a big impact on the clarity of your ideas.

Please use the provided rubric to make sure your response meets these common criteria. Try to have a friend or family member grade your response for you or take a break after writing your response and return to grade it with fresh eyes.

Constructed Response Rubric

Domain	Description
Content Knowledge	• The response directly addresses every part of the prompt. • The response demonstrates independent knowledge of the topic. • The response discusses the topic at an appropriate depth.
Organization	• The response introduces the topic, usually with a thesis statement or by restating the prompt. • The response directly addresses the prompt by providing a clear and concise answer or solution. • The answer or solution is supported by logical arguments or evidence. • The response restates the main idea in the conclusion.
Arguments and Examples	• The response provides a reasonable answer to the prompt. • The answer is supported by strong reasoning or evidence. • The response develops ideas logically and connects ideas to one another. • The reasoning and evidence provided act to support a unified main idea.
Language and Usage	• The response demonstrates effective use of grammar and uses varied sentence structure throughout the response. • The response demonstrates correct use of spelling, punctuation, and capitalization. • The response demonstrates strong and varied use of vocabulary relevant to the topic and appropriate for the intended audience.